Precious
Solitude

Precious Solitude

Finding peace and serenity
in a hectic world

Ruth Fishel

ADAMS MEDIA CORPORATION
Holbrook, Massachusetts

Published by
Adams Media Corporation
260 Center Street, Holbrook, MA 02343

ISBN: 1-58062-209-7

Printed in Canada.

J I H G F E D C B

Library of Congress Cataloging-in-Publication Data
Fishel, Ruth.
Precious solitude: finding peace and serenity
in a hectic world / by Ruth Fishel.
p.   cm.
ISBN 1-58062-209-7
1. Spiritual Life. 2. Women—Religious life.
3. Solitude—Religious Aspects. I. Title.
BL625.7.F54   1999
155.9'2—dc21   99-15772
CIP

Cover illustration by Vince McIndoe.

*This book is available at quantity discounts for bulk purchases.
For information, call 1-800-872-5627.*

Visit our home page at http://www.adamsmedia.com

Dedication

This book is dedicated to a very special woman. She is centered and peaceful, strong and wise, talented and creative, confident and curious, loving and compassionate, and spiritually connected to all the natural energies of the universe. She is alive and thriving within all of us; always there when we take time in precious solitude to find her.

❧ CONTENTS ❧

Loving Ourselves

A Time to Heal

Nature

Active Solitude

Inactive, Quiet Solitude

Activities for Peace and Renewal

Mini-Mental Retreats

Contemplation

Dear Reader,

Welcome to the wonderful world of solitude! Whatever your current relationship is with solitude, my hope is that *Precious Solitude* will bring you to a deeper knowledge of how important it is to all of us, to a fuller understanding of its rich rewards, and to ways to make it a regular part of your life.

Women are still the primary caretakers of children or parents, and yet a large majority of us also work, whether by choice or by necessity. Finding time alone is not an easy task. Yet it is an essential one if we are to keep our balance, grow as spiritual beings, and stay sane!

I was thrilled to be invited to write this book because it gave me an opportunity to explore further a subject I have valued ever since I was a young girl. The world has changed since then. Many of our lives are more complicated and full of stress, and taking time alone for ourselves is more important today than ever before.

To explore what solitude meant to other women, I developed a simple questionnaire. You might want to answer the questions on it yourself to become tuned into what solitude means to you before starting to read *Precious Solitude*. Review the questions again after you read the book to find out how your awareness of what solitude means to you might have grown.

Questionnaire

What does solitude mean to you?

Do you take time regularly to be alone? Yes__No__

If yes, how much time do you take?
Frequently__Rarely__Varies__Other?__

In solitude I usually feel:
Bored__Peaceful__Agitated__Frightened__It varies__
Other__

Do you prefer solitude to be active__inactive__both__

Would you like to increase__decrease__keep the
same__amount of solitude in your life?

What is your favorite way to bring solitude into your life?

The following questions can be answered yes if you feel you are
that way most of the time:

    Are you well-balanced?__
    Do you have peace in your life?__
    Are you content with your life?__
    Have you found your life's purpose (for now)? __.

What are (if any) the problems of solitude for you?

What don't you like about solitude?

Please share any obstacles you might have to going "inward"?

Can you share a particular time when solitude played an
important part in your life?

Has the meaning of solitude changed as you have matured?
How?

What does spirituality mean to you?

Do you consider yourself a spiritual person?

How do you know when you are getting answers from your soul, spirit, higher self, or God versus your mind?

What does it mean to you to go within?

I also had the privilege of interviewing many women personally who shared their thoughts, feelings, and experiences on the subject of solitude. Many of their answers and stories, as well as those of the women who answered the questionnaire, are sprinkled throughout the book.

Please join me as we discover or rediscover solitude. We'll explore its many faces and consider the numerous obstacles that often keep us from taking this precious time for ourselves. Finding new ways to go beyond these obstacles, we can see how solitude can help us to better know and understand ourselves, open our hearts to expand the love we have for ourselves, and deepen our connection with our spiritual selves, God, or any power, spirit, or supreme being in which we believe. We'll learn how healing can take place in solitude.

We seek solitude in countless ways and places. Solitude is not limited to whether or not we are active or still. Its meaning, too, varies from individual to individual, and what it means to us can change from day to day, depending on what is going on in our lives at any given time. What worked for us earlier last week might not bring us satisfaction this week. And what didn't seem fulfilling yesterday might be *just* what we need today.

The inner peace of solitude can be found while quietly stitching our family history on a tapestry, meditating in an

Ashram on the top of a mountain in Tibet, soaking in a tub, journaling, gardening, walking, writing, painting, reading, swimming, eating, hiking, going on a retreat with others or alone, or creating a personal retreat at home. These are only a few of the countless paths we can take to find precious solitude. There are many more suggestions to help you open your own door to peace.

Inner peace cannot magically appear when we are consumed with our daily activities, no matter how much we will it to be so. At some point we must make the decision to excuse ourselves from everyday life, walk away, close the door on noise and responsibilities, and spend some quiet time alone. Inactive solitude, such as meditation, prayer, contemplation, and simply being still, in contrast to being busy with solitary activities, is necessary. These spiritual paths can be relaxing and peaceful, insightful and enlightening, healing and restorative.

An affirmation for inspiration and empowerment is at the end of each section. You'll find suggestions for subjects to contemplate and activities to explore that can help you find peace and harmony, clear your path from any places where you might feel stuck, or simply help pamper yourself.

Solitude can be whatever you want it to be, for any purpose or no purpose at all. It can be a time for growing, learning, seeing, relaxing, accomplishing, contemplating, problem solving, meditating, praying , finding peace of mind, or just having plain fun!

May you continue to grow in richness and in peace as you discover new ways to include and enjoy precious solitude in your life.

With love and peace,
Ruth Fishel
Marstons Mills, Cape Cod, Massachusetts

Acknowledgments

I am deeply grateful to my partner Sandy Bierig for all her extraordinary patience, wisdom, and generous contribution of many, many hours of valuable editing and insights; for her ongoing support; and for her gift of solitude;

All the women who searched deep within their hearts and shared their experience, thoughts, and feelings with me in the questionnaires and interviews. I couldn't quote you all, but I want you to know that all your thoughts and insights are interwoven throughout the spirit of this book;

My daughters Debbie Boisseau and Judy Fishel for all their love and encouragement;

Readers Dorna Allen, Joseph Foote, Kathi Sommers, Barbara Thomas, Samatha White, and the women in my writer's group for their thoughtful feedback, support, and encouragement;

Margo Nash for her many hours of reading and rereading and her constructive editing and insights;

Anne Weaver, editor at Adams Media Corporation, for creating the idea and title for *Precious Solitude* and for having the confidence in my writing to invite me to write this book;

All my teachers Sylvia Boorstein, Christina Feldman, Joseph Goldstein, Narayan Liebenson Grady, Larry Rosenberg, and Sharon Salzman; and my special friends, authors and workshops leaders who have taught me so much.

PRECIOUS SOLITUDE

WOMEN NEED SOLITUDE IN ORDER TO FIND THE TRUE ESSENCE OF THEMSELVES: THAT FIRM STRAND WHICH WILL BE THE INDISPENSABLE CENTER OF A WHOLE WEB OF HUMAN RELATIONSHIPS.

ANNE MORROW LINDBERGH

Discovering Solitude

SOLITUDE—WALKING ALONE, DOING THINGS ALONE—IS THE MOST BLESSED THING IN THE WORLD. THE MIND RELAXES AND THOUGHTS BEGIN TO FLOW AND I THINK I AM BEGINNING TO FIND MYSELF A LITTLE BIT.

᠅ HELEN HAYES

When I was in grade school I loved to ride my bike to a beautiful estate a few miles from my home where I spent wonderful hours in solitude. I always brought a snack, a pen, a notebook, and a favorite book with me. As I entered the long driveway and passed the NO TRESPASSING sign, the caretaker would wave hello, knowing that I would cause no harm. I headed straight for my favorite place, a large pond filled with goldfish. A massive tree flourished beside the pond. The tree had a flat branch, wide enough for me to sit on, extended about ten feet out over the water. It was just high enough for me to swing my feet and not get wet. I sat there for hours reading or writing poetry, totally absorbed, completely content with my time alone. At other times, after school or on weekends, I climbed up to the flat roof of our apartment house where I spent hours happily painting pictures of nearby rooftops nestled among the tops of the trees.

Something deep within me guided me to these places. I never questioned whether I should be going there. I just knew it was where I belonged. I followed some inner guidance I did not understand at the time, and still do not completely understand now. I simply knew that was what I needed and wanted to do.

It was just as natural for me to go off by myself as it was to return to the team sports I loved equally well. I belonged to my school tennis, basketball, and field hockey teams and spent many joy filled hours in passionate competition with my classmates.

I remember that, at some point, my mother became concerned with the long hours I spent alone. She was worried that there was something wrong with me and wanted me to spend more time with other children. She thought I was unhappy. But I knew there was nothing wrong with me. I was following a natural rhythm of solitude and community, moving back and forth in a way that came very naturally to me.

As we grow older, life gets busier and filled with more demands and responsibilities. Precious times like those, the ones in our childhood, become less and less available to us. This does not mean that our need for solitude is any less important. We need to find the time for solitude in our lives. As Sarah Ban Breathnach writes, "Solitude is as necessary for our creative spirits to develop and flourish as are sleep and food for our bodies to survive."

It is time to explore the value of solitude in my life and what it means for me. No matter what is going on in my life, I am worth taking this precious time for me. ▩

Exploring Solitude

WITHIN OURSELVES THERE IS A DEEP PLACE AT WHOSE EDGE
WE MAY SIT AND DREAM.

✤ LEHRMAN

Let's discover and explore the joys of solitude, the precious, delicious experience of choosing to spend time with ourselves for a specific reason, or for no reason at all. We will look into the wonderful value of solitude in a world that is overflowing with too much to do and too little time in which to do it. We will discover ways to find the time, to take the time, and to value ourselves enough to know that we deserve the time for this precious gift.

In solitude we can find our authentic self, our true nature, our connection to each other and to God. We can discover where we belong in the universe and find our own true purpose. In solitude we can reach a place deep within where we can find peace.

Of course, the meaning and value of solitude vary from person to person. As we explore what it means to different women, we will find that our own perspective may expand. Discovering how other women describe their feelings, desires, and experiences about solitude may trigger new thoughts and emotions within us. It can help us to identify thoughts and emotions that we might never before have considered.

We'll go on to explore active and inactive solitude and the variety of ways we can experience being alone. We'll look at the many benefits of solitude and how it brings us closer to our true nature, to our fellow human beings, and to God. There are also exercises and suggestions to try, offering an opportunity to explore your own personal growth, healing, and transformation.

There are times when solitude is not always a choice, when living or being alone is not one's preferred lifestyle. Sometimes it is thrust upon us when least expected or desired. Yet, those times, too, can be powerful and healing if we learn to experience them as valuable lessons and to accept them as places we need to be at the time.

We will investigate the many, many, many, many obstacles to solitude and learn how to distinguish between those real and those imagined. By developing a deeper understanding of ourselves and how we relate to the world around us, we can discover how we can change and live a life of increased peace, balance, love, and joy. A variety of subjects will be suggested for contemplation such as creativity, balance, purpose, truth, personal values, family, love, and nature.

Welcome to a new and thoughtful journey. May it bring peace and joy to your life in ways you never thought possible.

I welcome solitude into my life today. I welcome the peace, serenity, wisdom, and spirituality I find when I take that special time for me. ▩

The Many Faces of Solitude

WHEN WE ALLOW OUR INNER SELVES TO BE HEARD WITHOUT BACKGROUND NOISE OR THE DIVERSIONS OF PROJECTS OR HOBBIES, WE WILL BEGIN TO DISCOVER THAT OUR INNER THOUGHTS ARE CREATIVE AND STIMULATING AND INTUITIVE. WE WILL BEGIN TO DISCOVER OURSELVES.

✣ AMY DEAN

Solitude can be delicious, comforting, enriching, healing, enlightening, and peaceful. It is so desired by many women that they make plans for months ahead just to have a few days alone. It can be a precious gift, an act of compassion we give ourselves. Solitude can be the glue that holds us together in an otherwise hectic, non-stop, often chaotic world. It can be our life preserver when we feel we are sinking into an ocean of overwhelming responsibilities and volumes of things to do.

However, at times, it is also multifaceted. Solitude can be depressing, undesirable, frightening, isolating, painful, revealing, and sad, with many gray areas in between. Any one of these feelings can be with us at any given time, only to be transformed in a heartbeat, as our thoughts, perceptions, and moods change.

Our goal is to discover where or when we can have the gift of all the positive aspects of solitude while accepting any of the less pleasant experiences with the knowledge that they will pass. For some, solitude might remain an enemy or an uninvited intruder. There certainly will be some periods in our lives when we choose not to seek solitude because we feel we are alone too much.

Others among us who seek the peace, comfort, and connection that solitude can bring to a busy and sometimes overwhelming world believe we can't have enough solitude.

There are times when we have too much solitude. Our job might keep us isolated and alone. Perhaps we work by ourselves or in a one-person office. We might be in a large room full of other employees, separated from each other by partitions so that we never feel connected to the rest of the staff. Sometimes we might come home to an empty house or live alone. We might become "hooked" on the Internet and spend hours alone at our computer, only to fall into bed alone and go to work the next morning still alone.

That is not to say that people living alone are necessarily sad. Living alone can be a choice, a conscious decision that fits someone for a particular time in life or maybe for always. After spending a life in marriage, the death of one's spouse or partner, or a divorce, many women decide that solitude is preferable for a while, maybe even forever. Some women no longer feel they must marry or have a partner. They feel complete in themselves.

During times when being alone is not our choice of how we want to live, we can still find happiness and joy in solitude. It can be used to produce clarity of mind, to examine oneself, or to experience personal growth. The result may be a new self-directedness and the courage to change what we can in our lives.

For women who are new to this concept, welcome to the priceless benefits of solitude, just waiting to be discovered. For women who know the precious gift of solitude, let these pages be your friend as you return again and again to find its treasure.

I look forward to solitude as a time when I can develop a deeper understanding of myself, including all the many facets that make up the complete and precious woman that I am. 🌺

Why Solitude?

MYSTICS, THROUGHOUT TIME, HAVE SPOKEN OF THE FREEDOM, WHOLENESS, LOVE AND COMPASSION THAT IS THE ESSENCE OF EACH OF US.

🌺 CHRISTINA FELDMAN

Women of various ages, interests, and backgrounds have shared with me why they value solitude in their lives, and the list of reasons is very long. The words peace, quiet, serenity, and contentment appeared over and over again. Among the others:

A time for inner reflection
A chance to connect with nature and my higher
　spirit
Time for my creative self
Renewing
Inner peace
One with God, time for God
Spaciousness
Stillness
Quietness
Time to just be
An opportunity to get in touch with my inner
　self and my God
Peaceful aloneness
Privacy
Being able to center myself
The absence of doing, not consciously accom-
　plishing anything
An opportunity to be still
Finding that deeper level of connection with
　God and feeling God's presence in my life
Focus on my priorities
Precious solitude is the quality time I spend
　with myself

A 52-year-old woman said, "In solitude I feel complete, contemplative, clear about my boundaries. I need to have 'down' time. I can be me, responsible to no one else in that time, except myself."

A 33-year-old wrote that it was a time when she could be herself and not put on any act to try to please someone else. "If I'm silly I can stay that way. If I'm angry, I can be angry."

A single parent said, "It's as important as breathing to me. One profound experience I had in my life was knowing the comfort of my own company."

An 18-year-old said it is "time to myself where I'm free to think and act as I please with no interruptions."

A pastoral psychotherapist describes solitude as a place where the different aspects of herself converge; the artist, the theologian and minister, the counselor, the woman alone, and the woman in a relationship.

A 42-year-old writer and holistic counselor said that solitude is either being alone or being in a state of mind in which she feels alone regardless of her surroundings.

A 37-year-old teacher said that solitude is a peaceful place where there is no one talking and the only person that needs her is herself!

And a 32-year-old lawyer said solitude was different things at different times. "At times solitude is loneliness, other times it is a chance to chill out and leave your troubles at the office."

Experiences with solitude were not all positive. One 47-year-old mother and owner of her own agency admitted that there are times in solitude when thousands of voices talk to her about her fears.

And while a 37-year-old literary agent usually feels relaxed in solitude, sometimes feelings of loneliness are present, or she has anxiety around work or her "to do" list.

A 54-year-old elementary school teacher said solitude can make her feel unsettled and overwhelmed, usually indicating that she is running from something or not staying in the present moment.

Yet there is not one woman I spoke to who did not see value in solitude. This is not to say that they all took time for it. Many barriers can be present to taking that time. We'll touch on that later.

It is time to explore what solitude personally means to me in my life today. ▩

Where?

"I love to sit on the beach and watch the sunsets, reflecting on the past and reviewing the various possible paths to the future. Somehow, I'm more objective when I'm at the beach. I can shut the rest of the world out and do my best inner reflection." This perspective came from a family nurse practitioner who found solitude to be a great help and comfort in her healing from the death of her husband.

An 80-year-old author finds solitude when she worships with her religious group. She feels a vibrant silence and describes the power like multiple batteries when people meditate together.

Another woman said that solitude included choosing what external stimulation she wants. "It's me making the choice of my environment." Often she chooses camping, where she hears the crackling of her campfire, the songs of the birds, the bark of coyotes, or perhaps even the growl of a bear.

One woman defined solitude as a state of mind. If we use that definition, solitude can be found anywhere, even in a crowd. Most of us, however, envision enjoying our precious solitude either in our own yard or away from our everyday life, traveling to some picturesque, pastoral scene, either alone or at a retreat where there are no interruptions, no noise, and no responsibilities.

Other women find solitude "sitting on my porch and watching the trees, birds and squirrels," "In hot baths in the candlelight," "With beautiful music," and "Running each morning through the woods."

The "where" of solitude can vary. There are times when everything falls into place: the finances, the babysitter, the job, the time. You can plan far in advance to go away to wherever your heart desires, whether it be the mountains, the ocean, the forest, or a secluded retreat.

Perhaps you have a room in your home where you can just chill out and spend time alone. Some women live alone and enjoy the solitude of their own days, doing whatever they choose to do. Others, though, live alone and at times find that loneliness creeps into their solitude. They ache for the company of a companion or mate.

Retreats offer wonderful opportunities for solitude and they can be structured or unstructured, according to your preference. There are retreat centers where you can pay for your room and food and spend the time as you wish. Other retreats are part of a program with others where you have both time alone and time with the group.

One of my favorite retreat centers is the Insight Meditation Society in Barre, Massachusetts, where I have attended two-, three-, seven-, and eight-day meditation retreats. They are held in complete silence, but for a fifteen-minute interview with the teacher and a forty-five minute discussion with a group each day. The rest of the time is spend in mindfulness and meditation. To set the tone for the experience, we are told in the beginning to keep our eyes downcast at all times, to avoid directly looking at anyone, therefore giving other people the respect of their own space.

Other times we can find solitude in gardening, boating, traveling, hiking, and simply sitting. We are not limited by where or how or when. Our only limitations are the excuses we give to ourselves and the restrictions of our own minds.

I am following my own inner path for solitude. I am going where my spirit leads me for peace and quiet and happiness. ▓

What Is It We Are Trying to Discover in Solitude?

LIFE IS ABOUT BEING REAL.

❧ FROM *THE VELVETEEN RABBIT*

Many times solitude has no special agenda at all. Those are the times when we aren't trying to solve or resolve anything. We are simply taking the time to be with ourselves. To be with whatever it is we discover. We just want to relax, get away from the turmoil of our daily routines, and rest within the silence. We want to renew, connect with our inner resources, and thus find serenity.

We can be surprised at times like these to find that while we weren't looking for anything, an inner voice nudges us to get our attention. It might speak to us in a whisper so faint we have to hold our breath to hear it or in a shout that really gets our attention. We will know when it happens. It might be something unfinished from the past. Perhaps it is time for a change that we have not yet been ready to make. Whatever comes up for us is where we are at that moment. Whatever comes up is ready for us to look at.

In solitude we can observe that we are prisoners to our own habits, fears, and conditioning. We see what has been holding us back and we can pray for the grace to be released from it although we might first have to pray to become willing before we can accept our freedom.

In the quiet of solitude we listen to the smiles as well as the tears in our hearts and become more and more familiar with the totality of our being. We truly come to know ourselves, all of ourselves, for the beautiful women that we are.

Today I will accept all that I see in solitude, becoming closer to my true essence, allowing myself to become more and more the beautiful woman God intended me to be. ▓

Forced Solitude

SOLITUDE IS SUCH A POTENTIAL THING. WE HEAR VOICES IN SOLITUDE WE NEVER HEAR IN THE HURRY AND TURMOIL OF LIFE. WE RECEIVE COUNSELS AND COMFORTS WE GET UNDER NO OTHER CIRCUMSTANCES.

❧ AMELIA BARR

While teaching meditation at Barnstable House of Correction I met Jane (this is not her real name). She was working very hard to control her temper. One day she lost it and was sent to solitary for five days. Solitary confinement is not a precious solitude! The cell is very small, with room for only a cot, sink, and toilet.

Telling me about her experience, Jane said that she was completely confined to that one room. She was lucky to have one book, the Bible, with her. Her first night she was restless and had to calm down her emotions, so she went about making her bed and talking to herself. "What's done is done," she said over and over again. The more she repeated this, the more accepting she became. Her mind and body became attuned to each other. As she completed her task of making the bed she stood on it and looked out the window.

The view from there was spectacular. Jane could see Barnstable Harbor. She sat on her bed Indian-style, facing the window and proceeded to thank her Higher Power. Tears started running down her face. "The joy and peace I felt inside were so strong. I continued to do this for the total time I was there. I kept quiet, listening to my inner being. What a difference I felt when I was released. What a joy it is to be without people and telephones. Just to reflect, calm the mind and body, to become one."

If we are very creative, when solitude is thrust upon us, we can use it to grow and change. Witness the many prisoners of war who have come out of solitary confinement with a deep faith.

When a child is out of line, he or she is punished with "timeout." The child is sent to the bedroom to be alone for a specific time, away from human contact. Sometimes the punishment turns out to be no punishment at all because children often end up playing with their toys or watching TV. To have the most value, it would be best if this time out was away from all distractions.

Shunning is used by some societies as a painful punishment. Children shun other children who are different. By not including them in their circle of friendship, they leave them painfully on the outside looking in, making them feel unacceptable and unworthy.

This can happen to anyone who is different, in the minority or in a society or family where they are powerless. Someone of a different skin color or religion or sexual orientation or a child with a physical or mental handicap can be the target for cruelty and shunning. Shunning is done by adults who lack compassion and understanding or who are fearful of someone who is not like them as well as by people who are basically insecure and look to others for approval.

Some religions go to the extreme and consider their children dead if the child goes against a religious law. There was a time in Orthodox Judaism when parents would not acknowledge the existence of a son or daughter who was gay or lesbian. The child was cruelly treated as invisible, left out of all family affairs, isolated, and ignored. Some churches excommunicate people who do not follow their rules.

My friend Samantha White suggests that our task is to learn that you don't have to be lonely just because you are alone. Perhaps when our solitude is not by choice, we can use it to find the value of solitude as an aid to growth and healing.

I can choose to turn any time alone into a spiritual experience. All I need is willingness. ✳

Clearing Up Words

LANGUAGE HAS CREATED THE WORD "LONELINESS" TO EXPRESS THE PAIN OF BEING ALONE, AND THE WORD "SOLITUDE" TO EXPRESS THE GLORY OF BEING ALONE.

❧ PAUL TILLICH

Alone, lonely, solitude, isolation . . . where does one word begin and the other end? My friend Margo Nash suggests that sometimes they exist separately and sometimes they exist all together. The words solitude and alone technically mean the same thing. When we are alone, we are in solitude. When we are in *solitude*, we are *alone*. It's the feelings the two words bring up for us that make them seem different.

The dictionary defines solitude as the quality or state of being alone or remote from society. Seclusion, privacy, hermitage, hiding, isolation, quiet, retreat, and retirement are all different states of solitude.

Loneliness can be part of solitude, too. The word lonely suggests a longing for companionship. When we are lonely, we do not usually wish to be alone. We are usually missing something or someone in our lives. Loneliness evokes pain.

The thought of being alone can bring up a variety of different feelings. When someone important to us dies, we are left alone, but it does not necessarily mean we are lonely. A daughter who has chosen not to marry and has stayed home for years to take care of her sick mother might feel alone and sad at the loss of her mother when she dies, but she may also feel a tremendous sense of freedom. On the other hand when a woman's life companion, her lover, her mate dies, she too is left alone. She suffers from tremendous grief and loneliness at the loss of her life partner, but there is no sense of freedom, only painful longing.

Isolation and seclusion both suggest shutting away or staying apart from others. Depending on the reason for it, people in isolation or seclusion might or might not be lonely. The feelings that arise in forced isolation can be fearful and depressing, but also peaceful. Isolation is often involuntary, as the isolation of a village in winter or of a patient with a contagious disease who is separated from others for their safety. Involuntary isolation has more to do with loss. Voluntary isolation has to do with solitude.

The major difference between all these words is in the way we feel when we hear them and how we respond when we are in that particular situation. We react from our own personal interpretation and from our actual experience with words such as isolation, seclusion, and loneliness.

Whether or not we choose solitude has a great deal to do with our feelings about being alone. When we choose to be ourselves, we can find pleasure in solitude. When we don't choose to be alone, such as when a lover, spouse, partner, or close friend dies, we probably would rather have these people around us. It is the opposite when someone dear to us walks out, or we are alone because of a divorce, illness, or natural disaster, and we are left feeling isolated and lonely.

The word *precious* means something that is highly prized, valuable, greatly esteemed, beloved, and cherished. When we put precious with solitude, we are talking about the joys of solitude. *Precious solitude* is an extraordinary state of being that brings us peace and contentment, balance and wisdom, healing and serenity.

Today I will take some time to reflect on the words lonely, isolated, alone, and solitude to see what they mean to me. Simply by taking this time out in my own day, I can find what is promised by precious solitude. 🪷

THE MANY OBSTACLES TO SOLITUDE

> *WE CANNOT LEAVE THE TRAP UNTIL
> WE KNOW WE ARE IN IT. WE ARE IN
> A NEEDLESS IMPRISONMENT.* ✖
>
> MARILYN FERGUSON

Overcoming Our Yesterdays

SOLITUDE USED TO MEAN FEELING ALONE, EMPTY, NOTHING. IT WAS A FRIGHTENING, SCARY FEELING. NOW SOLITUDE IS PEACEFUL AND CALMING.

✢ ANONYMOUS

So many obstacles stand in the way of taking time for ourselves. Each one of us has different sets of obstacles, depending on our life experiences and how we were brought up. Our religion, nationality, society, and even our neighborhoods continue to influence how we feel about ourselves long into our adulthood. The examples set by our own mothers or caretakers have a great impact on our willingness to take time for ourselves.

We carry messages from our childhood deep within ourselves. Perhaps we were told that we had to clean our rooms and do our homework before we could take time for ourselves. Maybe we had other jobs around the house or were responsible for our siblings. Perhaps it was necessary for some of us to work to help support the family, leaving no extra time for ourselves. Some of us were told very clearly that doing things for ourselves was selfish.

If we carry the message that we could do what we wanted only after everything else were finished, we really know that everything will never be finished. There will always be something else that needs to be done. There will never be time for us!

As adults we often allow our partners, children, and jobs to influence so many of our decisions, making the idea of solitude seem far out of our reach. Some of us let friends come before our own alone time.

By taking time for solitude we become more knowledgeable about ourselves. Gaining in our understanding of what is essential to our souls, We become stronger in speaking up for our needs, first to ourselves, and then to the people in our lives.

"If you want the kernel you must break the shell," notes Meister Eikart. The shell can be all the walls that we keep up to avoid knowing ourselves. It can be everything on our "to do" list, all our busyness, our fears and worries, our co-dependence, our perfectionism, our sense of self-importance, our indispensable sense that we are the only ones who can get the job done right. We are the kernel, the prize. Our lives are so special; each and everyone of us is special. We deserve this time for ourselves to get to know ourselves, to be our own best friends and to be connected with our inner spirits.

Anne Morrow Lindbergh warns us that all our busyness and demands in our lives lead to fragmentation. She writes that the life of multiplicity does not bring grace; it destroys the soul.

How do we take time if we don't think we deserve time? How do we take time if we don't put ourselves first? How do we let ourselves grow when we don't value the needs of our souls?

We do it by first making a decision, whether we believe we deserve to take time for ourselves or not. Simply by making this decision, we actually begin to change a negative thought in our subconscious. We begin to remove a barrier that has held us back from our authentic selves. This decision gives us personal power. We are choosing to take charge of our lives.

We say "YES!" to ourselves and follow through with action. We form a firm and clear intention. We do it a step at a time, a day at a time, a minute at a time.

Today I am putting all old messages aside and taking time for me. Even if it is only five minutes, I know I am worthy of this quality personal time. ▒

Conquering the Fear of Solitude

WHEN WE MAKE THE COURAGEOUS CHOICE TO BE STILL, RATHER THAN RUNNING AWAY, WE HAVE THE CHANCE TO ESTABLISH A RELATIONSHIP WITH WHAT IS.

❧ SHARON SALZBERG

Some women have a great fear of solitude. Painful memories can rise to the surface. Thoughts of old resentments, loss, abandonment, and disappointments can fill the empty space. Old traumas, abuse, and negative experiences might feel too painful to be relived. There is also fear that we won't be able to handle the emptiness or that we'll be bored without our comfortable activities.

Women who have been physically or sexually abused have great fear of memories returning when they are alone. They want to keep those feelings buried and hope they never appear. This is also true of the addict or the alcoholic in early recovery. Feelings of guilt and shame for all that has happened while under the influence of drugs or alcohol can feel too overwhelming to handle.

I remember a time many years ago when I was recovering from my own struggle with alcoholism. Driving alone one night the silence felt unbearable and yet I could not listen to the radio. Soft music triggered excruciating emotional pain and sadness, and I thought my heart would break.

Losses from death or abandonment that have not yet been grieved, block us from finding comfort in our time alone. Anger, resentments, regrets, and self-pity stand in the way of our being able or even willing to be alone with ourselves.

Often our "too busy" syndrome is a subconscious cover-up to keep us from feelings. We stay busy or keep ourselves numbed by drinking, drugging, staying sick, overshopping, exercising, gambling, or being depressed. All the time we are running in all directions "out there" and never stopping to look "in here."

However, there's an old saying that God never gives us more than we can handle, and I believe this to be true. Whatever is within us is eagerly waiting to be discovered, to be dealt with, and to be let go. Our pain will not disappear by itself. We can block it, hide it, or deny it, but only for the time being. At some level it is always there, a barrier to our freedom, a wall between ourselves and others, a rejection of our true spirit.

There is a wonderful Zen story that illustrates this so well:

> There was a man so displeased by the sight of his own shadow and so displeased with his own footsteps that he determined to get rid of both. The method he hit upon was to run away from them. So he got up and ran. But every time he put his foot down there was another step, while his shadow kept up with them without the slightest difficulty. He attributed his failure to the fact that he was not running fast enough. So he ran faster and faster without stopping, until he finally dropped dead. He failed to realize that if he merely stepped into the shade, his shadow would vanish, and if he sat down and stayed still, there would be no more footsteps.
>
> —CHUANG TZU

Sit down in the shade. Write about your feelings and your memories, talk to someone you can trust, find a good therapist, but don't keep on running. Stay still long enough to come to the place where there are no more shadows or footsteps.

Give solitude a chance. Know that you can be with your feelings. Make friends with them. Know that they are as much an important part of you as your good memories. Let your times in solitude help you to heal.

I know I have all the courage I need today to begin to take time for me. Fear no longer blocks me from getting to know myself. Today I dare to be with me and to be all that I am. ✺

Whatever Works for You

FEW FIND INNER PEACE BUT THIS IS NOT BECAUSE THEY TRY AND FAIL, IT IS BECAUSE THEY DO NOT TRY.

❧ PEACE PILGRIM

One late August Sunday I decided to take some time with solitude and take advantage of one of the last beautiful days of summer. I wanted to spend a few hours relaxing on one of my favorite beaches. In spite of occasionally squealing babies and a few loud conversations nearby, I was relaxed and completely absorbed in my book.

Suddenly I was shocked out of my concentration when I heard a telephone ringing. I couldn't believe it! I looked over toward the source of the intrusion violating my space. There sat a young woman in her beach chair, a few feet back from the water, with a telephone to her ear. To my amazement, no sooner had she finished her call and put her phone back in a tote bag when it rang again! My mind raced with upset, irritability, and anger. Didn't she want to relax? How could she be so thoughtless of those of us who did? I had a strong desire to go over and ask her how she could do this to herself and those nearby.

Fortunately for both of us, my mind went in another direction. I thought maybe she has a parent dying from cancer or a sick child at home. I, too, would want to have a telephone with me also if such a situation were happening in my life. Maybe this was her only day off, her only time to get away and have some solitude. Maybe this was the only time she could get a babysitter for her children or a nurse for her sick parent. Maybe the only way she could have peace of mind in her one hour of solitude was to bring her phone with her wherever she went.

It occurred to me that I could simply move to a quieter, less crowded place on the beach since my personal solitude was in jeopardy. Everything I had been feeling, all my unhealthy critical judgments (a trait I don't like about myself) began to melt away and were replaced by feelings of compassion and understanding.

Our lives are too important to wait until the time when we are free from crisis or have all the money we need, or whatever. Even if you must take a telephone into your space of solitude, do it. If it means putting off the payment of a bill for a few days to hire a babysitter, it's worth it.

No matter what is going on or isn't going on in our lives, we need to find a way to just be with ourselves, no matter what!

Time alone to nurture my soul is as important as food to nurture my body. Today I will find some time to be with me, no matter what!

Breaking the Cycle of Caretaking

*A MAN WORKS FROM RISING SUN TO SETTING SUN
BUT A WOMAN'S WORK IS NEVER DONE.*

✢ AN OLD, OBSOLETE SAYING

It seems as if caretaking has been the role of women to serve since Adam and Eve. Caretaking has been in our genes, a message passed down from mothers to their daughters and to their daughters and to their daughters, ad infinitum. That's why when women finally began to go to college in large numbers, many trained to become nurses and teachers. For the most part, it is only since the 1960s or the 1970s that women have gone beyond the conventional curriculum and entered into what has traditionally been "man's" work. Finally, more and more women are becoming corporate executives, physicians, lawyers, physicists, and even astronauts. The number of women entering politics is still small, but increasing all the time.

In the 1970s a wonderful, freeing bumper sticker appeared: "A woman's place is in the house . . . the White House," disputing this way of thinking. I smile when I see this freeing affirmation today.

For many years my mother came home, prepared supper and served it at three separate times, after working all day as a secretary. First she served my brother who needed to be at the gym for basketball practice; then she and I waited for my father, until we finally gave up and ate without him at 6:00 or 6:30. Eventually my father stumbled up the stairs after "stopping to have a few with the boys," after work and she served him his supper. Later in the evening she peeled an orange and cut up an apple for him. And this was after she had worked a full, hard day herself!

My friend Ann is a twin. She was always praised when she did something for her sister and told she was wrong when she didn't. If Ann bought something for herself, her mother asked her where one was for her sister. Her mother always said to everyone, "Look how much they do for each other. See how they look out for each other." One day Ann's four brothers gave her a pin with four medallions representing each brother. Excited, she ran to show it to her mother. "And where is the one for your sister?" she was asked.

Still, some of us were encouraged to be ourselves and go for what was in our hearts. Katherine Hepburn once said, "I never realized until lately that women were supposed to be inferior."

For those of us who did get the message to put others first, it's really hard to turn that around and give ourselves permission to put ourselves first. The old messages still linger. When everything else is done, we say, waiting for that day that never comes.

Willingness is the first step toward change. Slowly and gently we have to learn that it is perfectly okay to do good things for ourselves. We have to honor our own specialness, our own individuality. We have to listen to our inner spirit. We must believe in ourselves and our self-worth. Until we do that, there will never be time for ourselves!

Use the following affirmations. Add others that are right for you. Write them on file cards, carry them with you, tape them to the visor of your car or to your refrigerator. Say them over and over until you believe them.

"My own care is important to me today." "Everyone can do without me while I take some time for solitude." "I will be responsible for myself and let others be responsible for themselves." ▓

Daily Pressures

IT IS SO CLEAR THAT IT TAKES LONG TO SEE. YOU MIGHT NEVER KNOW THAT THE FIRE WHICH YOU ARE SEEKING IS THE FIRE IN YOUR OWN LANTERN, AND THAT YOUR RICE HAS BEEN COOKED FROM THE VERY BEGINNING.

❧ CHINESE POEM

Sometimes our activities can make us frantic. Without knowing it, we can let everyone and everything around us run us. The phone rings and we run to answer it. Bills pile up and we're stressed with worry. A child needs this or that. The school, library, doctor's appointment, work, church or temple, a neighbor, teacher, cousin, friend, mother, child, partner or spouse, everyone's demands can become more important than our own inner needs.

Many a day is non-stop, from morning to night until we fall into bed at night completely exhausted, without having had one moment to ourselves. This can be especially true when the children are very young, but just as demanding if you're in a stressful job, juggling work and children, in school, or combining school with work or family.

Why not make a decision to try a new way of dealing with your day. Decide to stop and bring your awareness to all your activities. Get out your notebook and jot down all your pressures. Each time a new demand, a new crisis comes up, ask yourself, "Do I really have to do this now?" When the phone rings, consider letting the answering machine do the work. If you're worried about the importance of the call, listen to see who is calling and then decide whether or not to pick it up. Or buy caller I.D. and know who the caller is immediately. Do I have to give in to a child's demand at this moment? Can the laundry wait until tomorrow? Does the house have to be cleaned up right now? If at work or school, examine whether better planning or self-discipline would take off some pressure. Ask yourself whether each demand is a must for right now.

Maybe the answer is yes to all the questions and there is nothing you can change. Maybe, for this time in your life, you have no choice but to be exhausted at the end of each day. By the very act of taking the time to stop and ask the questions, to examine what you do in each day, you are slowing down and turning off your automatic pilot. By simply not saying yes automatically to outside demands you begin to be in touch with and listen to your own inner spirit. You must slow down and listen to your inner spirit, the voice of your soul.

Times that you take for yourself in solitude help you to get in touch with your inner voice, so that you are more in tune with it all times. Then, in the busyness of everyday life, you will know when it says to you, "Stop. Breathe. Slow down. Take a moment to relax. Be gentle with yourself."

What we have been looking for all along has always been within us, we just have to stop long enough to find it.

Today I will examine all the demands and pressures, taking time to see when I am simply putting unnecessary pressure on myself. I am willing to let go of anything that really isn't important and take some special time for me. ✖

Busy Mind

HAPPINESS IS LIKE A BUTTERFLY, THE MORE YOU CHASE IT, THE MORE IT WILL ELUDE YOU. BUT IF YOU TURN YOUR ATTENTION TO OTHER THINGS, IT COMES AND SOFTLY SITS ON YOUR SHOULDER.

❧ NATHANIEL HAWTHORNE

One of the greatest obstacles to finding peace in solitude is the ongoing busyness of our minds. Some people do not even want to take time for solitude because they know that in the absence of activity, their busy minds can make them feel as if they are going crazy.

Our minds have been compared to monkeys, jumping from branch to branch to branch, doing whatever they want. There are times when we can not control our thoughts and they will, like monkeys, go wherever they want to go. Peace and quiet are not always ours for the asking. There are times when, as much as we look forward to our time alone, we end up disappointed by our busy, racing mind going from one thought to another or by our mind repeating the same thoughts over and over again.

If we continue to insist on happiness or peace as our only goal, we will be disappointed. By letting go of expectations and accepting whatever is going on in the moment, we can help to eliminate our frustrations. Simply watching our busy mind without judgment is one way to allow our suffering to pass.

Finding happiness in solitude might not always be possible. Sometimes it's good to let the fact that you are getting away and having a change of pace be enough. Settle for contentment. On a televison interview, singer Billy Joel said,

"Happiness is an extreme, just as sadness is an extreme. I think there's a lot to be said for contentment."

Even contentment is not always easy to find. We may need to experiment strolling down a variety of paths to discover the one that's right for our own inner peace. Some ways will take you there on one day but not on another. Be gentle with yourself. Accept when one way doesn't work and move on to something else. Our choices are only limited by our imagination and our willingness to try new things or to persevere with old ones. We can also make less active choices such as prayer, meditation, contemplation, or reflection.

Connecting with the rhythms of your breath can also break the busy mind patterns. Meditation is a wonderful technique to quiet your mind. Soft music, candles, and incense can also help to sooth the busy mind.

But what about the times when we want to stop our busy minds? Active solitude can be the answer. Physical activity is a wonderful way to get out of your head and into that wonderful peaceful state of being fully absorbed in something. Gardening, walking, jogging, chopping wood are just a few of the physically active things you can do. And for a more quiet time there is reading, cooking, sewing, painting or being absorbed in a crossword puzzle. There are so many ways you can find peace in solitude that can occupy your mind and keep it from its constant whirlwind.

Today I will remember the old saying: "Please God, don't let my thoughts disturb my peace of mind." I'll find activities I enjoy in solitude and relax and let go. ▓

Goodbye Errand Queen

*LIFE IS WHAT IS HAPPENING WHEN YOU'RE BUSY MAKING
OTHER PLANS.*

❧ JOHN LENNON

I used to wake up in the morning and even before even getting
out of bed think about all the things I had to do for the day. I
was tired without even moving my body. Before I learned a
better way, I would go over and over my "to do" list, and then
would work on my budgets. First there were the personal
budget and all the bills that had to be paid, trying to figure out
where the money would come from. Then the mental work for
the company budget began. In no time, I would become filled
with hopelessness and depression.

Next I would be off thinking about fund-raising ideas, creating letters and more lists in my head. Before long, my "to do"
list had grown even more overwhelming. Thank goodness for
prayer and meditation! For many years they have replaced my
first morning thoughts. I no longer dread beginning my day.

My friend Kathleen Royal e-mailed me one day that she
finally took some time to meditate and slow down. Having found
such peace in this choice, she wondered why she hadn't done it
more often. She concluded that it was because she was always so
busy in her mind. She knows the value of staying in the now and
celebrating the moment but her Errand Queen comes out and
takes control of any down time she took for herself.

"I know I give my power away to her," Lita e-mailed. "I'm
too responsible to just sit and be."

We all have an Errand Queen! That inner voice that tells
us we have too much to do! The trouble is we listen to her. And

if we continue to listen to her, we will never have a moment's rest. Because there will always be something else to do.

I remember a day when twelve boxes of greeting cards came in from the printer. The artist and I excitedly opened the boxes to see the final results of all our work. Then I hurried her out the door, because we had an appointment at the printer.

"But I want to take some time to look at them," she told me.

"If we don't go to the printer now and discuss holiday cards with them, our next season's cards won't be ready on time." I answered.

The disappointment on her face struck a chord somewhere deep within me. I still remember it. I knew there was a lesson there and I didn't want to see it at the time. Deep down I knew she was right, wanting to take some time to enjoy our work now. I was rushing off, already in the future, failing to appreciate the now. My Errand Queen was in charge of my now.

How many times have you completed one task and had a momentary sense of satisfaction, only to have that space filled with more things that you must do? And where does "must do" come from? Isn't it our own inner Errand Queen that tells us we must do this or that now?

One of my favorite sayings is "How important is it?" By asking this question when you say you haven't time for solitude, you can say goodbye to your Errand Queen and enjoy the extra minutes that can pile up in your day!

Today I am willing to let go of my Errand Queen and take a good look at what is really important in my life. I know I have a choice today and can put myself high on my "to do" list. ▓

The Wonderful Tool of Noting

WHEN WE LET GO OF OUR BATTLES AND OPEN OUR HEARTS TO THINGS AS THEY ARE, THEN WE COME TO REST IN THE PRESENT MOMENT. THIS IS THE BEGINNING AND END OF SPIRITUAL PRACTICE.

JACK KORNFIELD

I become very creative when I am taking a trip on an airplane, often writing nonstop for hours. The distractions from home and office are left behind and I can be very single focused. On one trip the man in the seat behind me was playing a radio. I was upset, wishing the stewardess would come back and tell him to turn it off. "Didn't he know you are not supposed to play a radio on a plane?" I thought, struggling to get back to concentrating on what I had been writing.

Fortunately I remembered the technique of noting or labeling as it is also called. In mindfulness or insight meditation we learn to label our thoughts as they appear in our minds and then go back to our breathing. By labeling them, or naming them, we are acknowledging and accepting them, rather then resisting or fighting them. An example of this is when a thought or a plan comes into our mind, we simply say, "thinking" or "planning." For some reason I have yet to understand, the thoughts immediately lose their power over us and our mind becomes empty again, even if it is for a brief time before the next thought appears.

By practicing this technique during our daily meditation, we can learn to bring it to each moment of our day, which keeps us in the present moment. After several minutes of frustration over this passenger's radio, I realized I was creating my own suffering. "What would I tell a student under these circumstances?" I questioned myself. "Of course! I would remind them about noting!" So I thought, "Disturbing music," and "Interruption" and after a moment, I was no longer aware of the music and became completely absorbed with my writing.

Noting or labeling is a wonderful technique to use in solitude when you become disturbed by a mind that won't give you peace. When the "to do" list won't leave you alone, just say "thinking" or "busy mind," and watch the thoughts disappear. Jack Kornfield writes, "Naming the difficulties we encounter brings clarity and understanding and can unlock and free the valuable energy locked up in them."

It also works if you can't fall sleep at night. There was a time when my thoughts kept me awake for a long time. When I learned this technique, I finally found a way to stop my circular thinking. I learned that it is impossible to have two thoughts at the same time. Therefore, when I breathed in I thought the word "peace," and when I breathed out I thought the word "tension." If I was nervous about something I thought the word "faith" when I breathed in and the word "fear" when I breathed out. Within minutes I was asleep.

By accepting and noting what is going on in the present moment I am finding peace in the present moment. I'm letting go of all my struggle to change what I cannot change! ▨

Be Where You Are with What You Have

*A LIFE OF JOY IS NOT IN SEEKING HAPPINESS, BUT IN EXPERI-
ENCING AND SIMPLY BEING WITH THE CIRCUMSTANCES OF
OUR LIFE AS THEY ARE; NOT IN FULFILLING PERSONAL
WANTS, BUT IN FULFILLING THE NEEDS OF LIFE; NOT IN
AVOIDING PAIN, BUT BEING IN PAIN WHEN IT IS NECESSARY
TO DO SO.*

✤ CHARLOTTE JOKO BECK

Sometimes we want to avoid taking time in solitude because
we might be experiencing deep, heavy, painful, or uncomfortable feelings. Perhaps we have suffered a loss from death or
divorce. Possibly we have received the sad news that a dear
friend or relative is sick or that we have a serious illness with a
bad prognosis. Maybe our feelings are hurt, we harbor some
resentment, and are full of rage.

Who wants to be alone with feelings like these, we ask,
willing to do almost anything to make them go away so we can
feel better. The fact is that by experiencing our feelings just as
they are, we will find peace more quickly than if we try to
avoid, change, deny, or hide them. A walk alone on the beach, a
quiet time at sunset, an entry in our journal are a few of the
ways that can help to ease our pain. Being in nature, seeing
that we are a part of a larger picture and that we are not alone
can lift the weight off our shoulders.

Author Jack Kornfield tells us that the true path to libera-
tion is to *let go of everything.* "Spiritual practice will not save us
from suffering and confusion. It only allows us to understand

that avoidance of pain does not help." He teaches that we must be mindful of the closed areas of ours lives, find in ourselves a willingness to go into the dark, and enter each place of fear.

Elizabeth Kubler-Ross lets us know that it's okay not to be perfect. She said, "I'm not okay. You're not okay. And that's okay."

F. Scott Peck opens his bestselling book *The Road Less Traveled* with the famous line "Life is difficult." This book has sold millions of copies, letting countless numbers of people know that they are not doing something wrong when they suffer, that they are not different. The Buddha teaches that suffering is inevitable. The avoidance of suffering and pain prolongs suffering and pain. The Bible tells many stories about how Christ ministered personally to those who suffered.

Love and compassion begin with ourselves. By avoiding being alone with our feelings, we lose a wonderful opportunity to get to know ourselves in all situations. We don't get to see that we can be okay with not being okay. The more accepting we are of all that is going on in our lives, the more gentle and loving we become with ourselves. We can learn to open our hearts to our pain as well as our pleasure.

Feelings are the barometer that give us valuable information on where we are mentally, emotionally, and spiritually. We can use this information to help to change the direction of our lives. Turning our feelings or situation over to our higher power in prayer and meditation can bring tremendous relief.

Today I am going to let this prayer be my inspiration: "Let me not pray to be sheltered from dangers, but to be fearless in facing them. Let me not beg for the stilling of my pain, but for the heart to conquer it. Let me not crave in anxious fear to be saved, but hope for patience to win my freedom." ▩

—THE PRAYER OF THE BODHISTAVA

Wasting Precious Time

I MUST GOVERN THE CLOCK, NOT BE GOVERNED BY IT.

❧ GOLDA MEIR

How often have you said that you don't have time to get away, that you just can't afford the luxury of taking time for yourself? How often do you think that there just isn't enough time in the day to do everything you think must be done? Notice that I wrote "you think must be done," rather than "must be done."

One of the biggest obstacles for taking time for solitude is that people say they don't have enough time. Maybe it's time to look at your daily routine and see if it's really necessary to do everything you are doing. It's helpful to get a notebook and, for one full week, write down everything you do each day. Next to each item, jot down the time that it takes to accomplish it. At the end of the week you can analyze your activities and see where you can cut out or speed up what is on your list.

Would it be more helpful to make a bigger shopping list and shop less frequently? Can you pay your bills once or twice a month, rather than at random? Perhaps you can pay your bills on line, or by phone, saving not only time but money for envelopes and postage. Can your kids or partner or spouse do more in the house? Can you join a car pool rather than driving alone?

Five minutes here and ten minutes there can add up to an hour you never expected, just for you.

Terry trades babysitting with another mother so she can have two hours a week to herself. She spends this time driving around accomplishing all the errands that take four times as long when she has to haul her little boys with her. "I love to drive along in silence, not even a radio playing. Those two precious hours are all mine. No one talks to me, demands of me, climbs on me, screams at me, fights around me, or needs me. When I return to pick up my sons I have renewed patience and I am a better mother."

I am adding up five minutes here and five minutes there and lo and behold I have more precious time for me! ▩

Energy Drainers

SAYING NO CAN BE THE ULTIMATE OF SELF-CARE.

✤ CLAUDIA BLACK

Have you noticed how, when you are with some people, you feel drained, as if your energy has been depleted? Some people take more than they give to you. They are energy drainers, people with negative energy who can pull you down. They are super needy, perhaps critical and judgmental. They are often complaining that nothing is ever right, and that people are always taking advantage of them. They believe their problems are always someone else's fault. They are wonderful at making you feel guilty if you don't give them what they want. And they are very subtle. You barely know you are caught in the trap until you are buried in it. They want your time, attention, or money, leaving very little left over for you.

If you have an idea they are quick to tell you everything that can go wrong, all the reasons that you should not go ahead with it. A friend told me these people are called bubble bursters in her sales organization. When you're feeling high on an idea, they stick a pin in your bubble to burst it. These are the people to stay away from. They drain your time and energy.

Other friends add to your energy and you feel good when you are with them. They give as well as take, encourage you to grow, and are there for you when you are in need. These are the people with whom to spend time.

Saying no is another way to save time. You can get caught up so easily joining clubs and organizations, all for a good cause. You make commitments to go to meetings and serve on committees. Examine how much time this takes up in your life and think about what is really important to you now. What could you let go of that could give you an extra thirty minutes for yourself each week. And yes, you are just as important as the organization. I am not suggesting that you shouldn't make a contribution to your community. Simply look at all that you do and see if there is an area that helps to make your life too cluttered and adds too much pressure to your days.

Procrastination is another energy drainer. Everything you put off adds stress to your life. When you know you need to do something, whether it is returning a library book, paying a bill, or having the roof repaired, you feel the burden of it. Whether you're conscious of it or not, you are carrying this list with you, slowing you down, draining your energy, making you feel less about yourselves, and holding you back from taking quality time for yourself. As these things stay undone on your "to do" list, you think you don't have time for solitude.

Why not take out your notebook and make a list of all the things that drain your energy. Awareness is the beginning of change.

Today I will bring my awareness to all the peoples, places, and things that drain my energy. I know I can make changes that will increase my energy and help me to find more time for myself! ▓

Giving Ourselves Permission

WE ARE ALL SEARCHING FOR PEACE,
BUT NOBODY SEARCHES FOR IT WHERE IT IS.

❧ SPANISH PROVERB

So many times the outdoors call to me while I'm working. My office is my home in a wonderful room full of windows that provide me with spectacular views of my backyard woods. I feel as if I am in a nest of leaves, with wonderful green oak and sycamore leaves everywhere I look. Everyday is different as the leaves go through their cycles of change.

On one particularly magnificent June day, following days of rain and clouds and gray skies, I found myself actually in physical pain. My body ached to be out in the air. I felt as if I were being drawn out of my chair. Still, I resisted, because I had a great deal to do that day.

One of my favorite sensations is to stop and take some time feeling the breeze against my skin, The irony is that I wait all winter for perfect days like this one. When it finally arrives, I tell myself I am too busy to enjoy it. In the end I had only wasted time with my inner battle, not accomplishing anything at all. Not being outdoors. Not working. Just struggling.

How many nights have I worked late? How many weekends have I put on retreats and workshops, only to go on and work the following week without a break? That was the way I justified giving myself permission finally to take some time off and go outside. I could smell the grass and the flowers waiting for me as I sat there.

Finally I shut down my computer and changed into shorts to go outside. I knew that a wonderful walk and a quiet time in my garden would energize me and I would return to my work content and grateful. But it was not meant to be. During the time I had spent struggling with the decision to go or stay, clouds had begun their unwelcome visit to block out the sun. It was no longer a beautiful, inviting June day. Happily, the phone rang, advising me of a problem with the pages of a cookbook I was publishing for a friend. In the end I settled for a ride to the printer with my convertible top down, grateful for a chance to be in the fresh air.

Whether we work for ourselves or someone else or have responsibilities as a mom, student, or caretaker, it may be just as difficult to leave and follow the call of our soul. Many of us think that peace is for later, when we are older. When the kids are grown, after graduation, when the better job comes, when the cleaning person can be hired, or when there's more money. Our lives become focused on studying or making money or creating the future, rather than developing the inner skills that bring us true happiness and peace in this present moment.

Whatever the reasons that hold us back, there comes a time when we just have to ignore all the old messages and decide to create new ones. We can even give ourselves permission to change our jobs, if at all possible. Karuna Kress suggests that we find work that has flexibility, so that we have more time for ourselves. We have to give ourselves permission to do something good for ourselves each day. We deserve to take time for ourselves.

Today I give myself permission to follow the calling of my soul. No matter what my head tells me, I'm following my heart. 🕸

GETTING
TO KNOW
OURSELVES

But where was I to start?
The world is so vast, I shall start with
the country that I know best, my own.
But my country is so large, I had better
start with my town. But my town, too
is large. I had best start with my street.
No: my home. No: my family. Never
mind. I shall start with myself. ▨

ELIE WIESEL, *SOULS ON FIRE*

Discovering Me

ALL THAT YOU WANT TO BE YOU ALREADY ARE.
ALL YOU HAVE TO DO IS MOVE YOUR AWARENESS THERE
AND RECOGNIZE THE REALITY OF YOUR OWN SOUL.

❧ JOHN-ROGER

I have heard our lives compared to the layers of an onion. It has been said that as we peel off the layers that hide us from our true selves, we come to the core of who we really are. A dear friend changed this image for me a long time ago to that of a rose, with all its beautiful, soft, and silky petals embracing the essence of whom we are.

Recently the image of an artichoke came to me. The leaves have sharp, painful points at their ends while the meat on the underside is tasty. The meat from the largest top layers has a tendency to be tough. As we continue to peel away the larger leaves of the artichoke, we find more leaves on each subsequent layer. When all the leaves are finally removed, we uncover a delicious treasure, the sweetest and most tender part of the artichoke, the heart.

No matter how well we think we know ourselves, there is always more to learn. The more we take time alone with ourselves, the more we discover. Dare to take that time alone! Discover the richness of all that you are. Uncover the layers of false impressions, fears, and other blocks to finding the real you. Search deep down for that loving, creative spirit that has been you all along.

The following pages in this section can be an inspiration for you to try on new ideas. Perhaps there are things you might have wanted to do but, for whatever reason, didn't dare attempt. Maybe fear stood in the way. Perhaps a parent pushed you in another direction. Or you thought you weren't good enough to paint or sing or write.

So reach into your own inner heart. Slowly peel off each leaf, layer by layer. Chances are you'll find something that has been holding you back from feeling free to go deeply into your own heart and find the precious you.

Today I will reach deeply inside of myself, under all the layers that block me from seeing the best of who I really am, and let me rediscover, again and again, my heart. ✠

Breathing Space

IF YOU CAN'T BUILD TEN MINUTES OF QUIET TIME INTO YOUR DAILY SCHEDULE, IT'S TIME TO FACE THE MUSIC: YOU'RE LOSING YOUR MIND, IF NOT YOUR SOUL.

❧ MILLER

Once there were two very tall and graceful birch trees growing in the front of our home that swayed back and forth with the wind. Their trunks were so close together that you could barely see the light between them. They could be mistaken from a distance for one tree with two tall branches. A baby birch tree sprouted and forced its way up in the inches between the two trees. One year, in a severe winter storm, the wind bent them over. Heavy wet snow stuck to their trunks. The wind held them bent almost to the ground until the sun melted the snow and they could stand tall and straight again. After that storm, whenever the wind blew hard, the trees, now weakened, bent over and swayed, brushing against the side and windows of our house.

I loved those birch trees. They gave me great pleasure, often reminding me of happy times at camp as a child. But I knew that they might damage the house and should be taken down. A few years went by as I continued to resist losing them, the noise of their scraping getting stronger and stronger with each passing winter. Finally, I gave in and made the phone call, steeling myself for the loss.

I watched, heartbroken, as the trees came down. When it was all over, the sapling, no more four or five feet tall and very thin because it had been wedged between the two, stood frail and alone. It took up no more than two or three feet in width. Within hours this width grew larger as the young tree was now able to spread its branches. It was taller by two or three feet within days. After two months this amazing tree added five more feet to its height and its branches stretched out over an eight-foot area. I would not believe this if I had not been there to watch this wonder. It now had the space to be the tree it was created to be.

When we don't take time for ourselves, when we scrunch ourselves into everyone else's schedule, squeezed by everyone else needs and demands, we can't grow to our full potential. The shadows of the people who run our lives block us, leaving us unfed and starving. The sapling was not capable of moving away to grow in the sun. It finally thrived when the mature trees were no longer there, as they had thrived when they unknowingly suppressed the growth of the sapling.

We don't have to leave those people we take care of or change jobs so that we can grow and flourish. We can step out into our own sunlight, take time to be alone, nurture our souls, and renew our spirits. We can get to know ourselves when we are not held back, overwhelmed and overloaded. Then, when we do return to our responsibilities, we are stronger and more independent. By finding time for our own breathing space, we are moving towards our full potential.

Today I will take time to make space for me to blossom. Nothing can stop me today from growing into the beautiful woman I was born to be!

Creating Your Own Special Space

YOU MUST HAVE A ROOM, OR A CERTAIN HOUR OF THE DAY OR SO WHEN YOU DO NOT KNOW WHAT WAS IN THE MORNING PAPER . . . A PLACE WHERE YOU CAN SIMPLY EXPERIENCE AND BRING FOR WHAT YOU ARE, AND WHAT YOU MIGHT BE.

JOSEPH CAMPBELL

My house sits on a lovely piece of land surrounded by woods, with a small pond on the back edge that feeds into a cranberry bog. We finally managed to clear away enough poison ivy on the path going down to the bog. In the circle of trees near the pond's bank we put up an inexpensive twelve-by-twelve screen room. We leave two chairs in the middle of the room, waiting for one or both of us.

This little screened room has added a whole new dimension to my life. It has given me a home away from home, a new place for solitude, where I can separate myself from computers and telephones. I can leave my cluttered office with papers piled and spread everywhere, which always remind me of things I need to do. Here I can come with just one thing or nothing. I can sit and stare or I can write. I can meditate, pray, read, and think, but I can do only one of those things at a time, in contrast to the office where I'm tempted to do everything at once.

The air there smells of Sweet William and there is a beautiful breeze on all sides since there are no walls to block it out. The trees rustle in beautiful, soft melodic rhythm. There are no telephones to block the song of the cardinals and finches, and all is right with the world.

The floor of my new room is a thick mulch of dried leaves built up over many years. It makes a natural, soft carpet for my hot, tired feet. I let my eyes go wherever they want. First they roam the floor that took nature so many years to create. Then my eyes wander across the many root systems of bushes, sycamores, and oaks that fashion a design of their own, weaving in and out, continuing on to the rest of God's magnificent landscape that surrounds my new room.

Swallows glide over the surface of the pond, turning and swooping in their graceful dance as they catch unsuspecting insects for dinner. A breeze sweeps across the water, creating ripples that disappear as quickly as the reflections of the leaves. Crows call. Bluejays screech and a graceful catbird watches me watching her. Dragonflies sweep gracefully over the pond as beautiful butterflies flutter in and out of view. I watch a green inchworm make her way along my arm. Before I brush her off I offer full assurance that I won't hurt her. All this, the wonder of nature, is in my own backyard.

There's not a better way to really get to know yourself than when you have a special place you can call your own. You can go there for a while and be completely yourself, doing something or nothing.

If at all possible create a special place for yourself. It can be a place shared with someone else, but somewhere that will allow you to be alone. It doesn't have to be an entire room; it can be a small section of a room, even a corner, a chair at a window or on a porch. This can become your own special place and you can feel vibrations of peace and serenity when you are near it. Eventually you will find this same peace and serenity simply by thinking about it.

There is a perfect place just for me where I can be alone and do anything I want to do. It's just the right size to give me all the comfort and peace I need.

Our Changing Needs

THE SOUL IS VERY CLEAR THAT ITS PURPOSE IS EVOLUTION.

NEALE DONALD WALSCH

When I was eleven years old, we moved to what was described as a "rich" neighborhood. Everyone else owned a single home. Ours was the only two-family rental on the block.

All the other families sent their children to summer camp, while my parents couldn't afford to send my brother and me. That first summer we had no one to play with because all the neighborhood kids were at camp. Although I know it was not intended by my parents, I grew up with the internalized image of my being "less than," not "as good as" others, an image which took me many years to change.

My mother was determined that we would not spend another summer without friends. She found a job at a camp as a dietician, a job she knew nothing about, so my brother and I could spend our summers there at a very reduced rate. Then, for the following four summers, Mom worked as secretary to the camp director, a job she was more comfortable in because that was what she was trained to do. My father came up on weekends to visit.

I spent the happiest times of my childhood at camp where I felt safe to be totally me. All my feelings of inadequacy, low self-esteem, and painful shyness vanished. I did what came most naturally to me, participating in sports. At home, I always struggled to keep up with everyone else, wanting to be accepted and part of a group in which I felt I was the outsider. I will be forever grateful to my mother for working those summers so my brother and I could have such wonderful experiences.

One beautiful, sunny summer day, on parents' visiting day, when I was twelve years old, I remember my father sitting on a swing on the camp's beach, gently moving back and forth. I can still see myself as I ran busily up and down on the sand, in and out of the water. At one point I came back to visit with my father and asked him how he could simply sit on the swing and do nothing. Wouldn't he like to go swimming? Wasn't he bored?

"I've been working hard all week and sitting quietly is exactly what I want to do," he explained.

"But how can you just sit there?" I pushed.

"Someday you'll understand," he answered.

I remembered his words years later when I had my own family and when all I wanted was to find the time to do nothing at all. Oh to find that swing on a beach, glide gently back and forth, simply watching the water coming in and going out, finding peace in the gentle quiet of the moment!

The need and desire for solitude are different for everyone. It changes for each person from year to year and even from day to day. It depends not only on our ability to include time for solitude in our lives, but also on many other factors. One's age, job, family situation, physical, mental and spiritual well-being, and financial conditions can all be factors.

Women with high self-esteem and self-confidence have a better chance of realizing the value of solitude and knowing they are worth finding a way to take time for it in their lives. Those with low self-esteem might not think they are worth it and therefore might have difficulty enlisting help from anyone to make it possible.

Know that we're all worth it!

Today I will re-examine the importance of solitude in my life. If I am not meeting my needs, I will take time to make a new plan to find regular time for me. ▨

Negative Beliefs

HUMAN BEINGS HAVE AN INALIENABLE RIGHT TO INVENT THEMSELVES; WHEN THAT RIGHT IS PRE-EMPTED, IT IS CALLED BRAIN-WASHING.

✳ GERMAINE GREER

Millions of dollars are spent advertising diet plans each year. Millions more are spent telling us how we should look. We should be fatter or thinner or blonder. We should wear this or wear that or the next thing so we will be popular or successful or "in" with the crowd. Louise Hay calls this the "I'm not good enough" advertising aimed at women, resulting in our accepting negative beliefs about our bodies.

In response to this pressure, many of us turn ourselves over to doctors to transform our outer self. Breast implants, liposuction, face lifts, and hair implants are but a few of the changes we make to look better on the outside. We think we will be happy if we simply change how we eat or dress or look.

How can we know who we really are when we listen to the messages about whom we should be? There's nothing wrong with changing how we eat if it will help us be healthier or changing how we look with a new haircut or new styles of clothing if we think we look better. Chances are we will never look like the model or movie star on the front page of a leading magazine. Nevertheless, that doesn't make us "less than" that star.

Let's remember what Eleanor Roosevelt wrote. "No one can make you feel inferior without your consent."

I will take time alone to take a good look at me, putting aside all the messages of how I should look, act, and think. I know I am on a path to self-discovery. As I continue to uncover the layers of "shoulds," I come closer to knowing my own inner beauty. ▨

Finding Our Own Answers

IF YOU DO NOT GET IT FROM YOURSELF,
WHERE WILL YOU GO FOR IT?

❧ THE ZENRIN

We can attend hundreds of workshops and read countless books and still not know what is right for us. Authors and workshop leaders can only be guides for our own personal exploration. Wise therapists only point the way and help us to ask the right questions. They can offer techniques, suggestions, teachings, and ideas. They can provoke thoughts and heighten our awareness. I in the last analysis, all answers lie within us. Only we know our own truth. Only we can answer our own questions.

Louise Hay, in her book *Empowering Women*, suggests a wonderful affirmation to say to ourselves when we want to connect with our Inner Resources and our Universal Connection—that Great Central Source of all life, as she calls it: *"I now go to that place within me where there is infinite wisdom; the answers I seek are within me."*

Louise tells us that we just need to create the opportunity by sitting quietly and connecting with the treasures within us. "It is vital that we give ourselves the time to listen to our inner wisdom. No person can be totally in touch with the abundant knowledge within, without taking time each day to meditate."

I can still walk past a section of new books in a bookstore and a sense of excitement rises in me when I see titles such as *The Seven Habits of Highly Effective People* by Stephen Covey or *The Seven Spiritual Laws of Success* by Deepak Chopra. I think, maybe this is something I missed or maybe this is finally it, the answer to perfect happiness. If I learn these seven simple truths my life will be perfect! I can still be ready to look for the easy way, the sure way, someone else's way. Like workshops and therapy, books can be a guide. Eventually we have to stop and find our own answers.

The book *Emanual* I tells us to listen with our heart. That is where our light and truth lie. "Once you begin to trust your heart you will realize that when something brings you joy and fulfillment it is the will of God speaking through your heart."

In solitude we can tune into our inner knowing by simply sitting still and being in touch with the truth that has always been there. Answers do not always come on call just because we want them. In meditation we create the space for them to grow. Like preparing the ground in our garden before we plant our seeds, the quietness of solitude prepares the ground for us to grow closer to the intuitive knowing of our souls. Like seeds lying dormant until the season is right to bloom, so do our questions wait for the right time to reveal the answers we seek.

In quiet meditation I will ask my questions, knowing that answers will be there when the time is right. ❋

False Evidence Appearing Real

COURAGE IS FEAR THAT HAS SAID ITS PRAYERS.

❧ PROVERB

In the 1950s, the general thinking was that women married right after college. It was said that girls went to college to "catch a man," but if they did choose to have a career, the traditional career was teaching or nursing. I was fortunate in that my parents encouraged me to expand my self and try other things. A few of my braver friends considered going to California after college. This was before California and "doing one's own thing" were the things to do. The idea sounded exciting, but when I mentioned this to my parents, they became quite upset.

"Your mother will die if you go to California," threatened my father, becoming more and more angry as I continued to push for permission. "She'll die of bleeding ulcers!"

When my mother heard my plans, she became quiet and withdrawn. Her long, thin, sweet face seemed even longer as she withdrew into a veil of sadness. My mother didn't even have ulcers, let alone bleeding ulcers, yet the fear that there could be the smallest chance that she might die because of a decision I made, the possibility that I could be responsible for her death were more than I could bear.

After promising never to mention California again, I received a three-page letter from my father, enthusiastically extolling the greatness of our country because its people had the courage to take an unpopular stand and fight for what they believed in, no matter what. "Where is that great spirit of yours? What do you mean you will never mention California again?" he shouted at me in his letter. This time I could only imagine his reddening face as be became more and more angry. I shook my head in disbelief. Confused and defeated, I began, unknowingly, to harbor a resentment against him that would take many years to heal.

Over time my father's anger intensified as his drinking accelerated. Life did not go the way he wanted it to and he become more and more depressed and often flew off into rages. My mother struggled with the decision to leave him and went to a social worker for advice. This young social worker asked her if she could handle it if my father took his life because she left him. The answer to this question bound my mother to my father until the moment she died.

She didn't dare to leave my father. I didn't dare to go to California. We both chose to stay, threatened with the possibility of someone dying because of our decision. How powerful we thought we were, and how very fearful; and how much power we gave to others. I didn't understand until many years later, through therapy, how much I was influenced by my father's threatening statements; and how confused I always felt when I had to make an important decision.

It's been said that fear is *False Evidence Appearing Real.* Imagine coming to the end of your life and someone finally tells you that all the fears you carried with you since childhood were just that, *False Evidence Appearing Real.* What a waste that would be. What we feared in childhood still holds us back until we are willing to look at it. Fear blocks us from seeing our strengths and our assets. Fear chokes our talents. Fear denies us the ability to love ourselves.

Our "what if's" hold us back. Fearing that the outcome will not be positive, we can miss many great opportunities in our lives. What are your "what if's?" *False Evidence Appearing Real* runs your life?

I will no longer let my fears block me from the person I'm supposed to be. As I take more time for me, I can grow in the willingness to move past my fears and grow in my faith. ✹

Our Own Ebb and Flow

YOUR HAND OPENS AND CLOSES, OPENS AND CLOSES.
IF IT WERE ALWAYS A FIST OR ALWAYS STRETCHED OPEN,
YOU WOULD BE PARALYZED.

❧ RUMI

In Chatham, Massachusetts, angry storms pound at the sand, which has been supporting homes looking out at the ocean. Eventually the waves wear down the sand, washing away the foundations on which people built these homes. One by one many tumbled into the sea like toy houses. The beaches become smaller and smaller, while simultaneously a new peninsula is slowly forming as this same sand is being washed into an inlet many miles away.

Nothing stays the same. As the tide changes by nearly an hour each day, our needs change as well. When we listen deeply, we can hear when our own needs change. We will come to know when it is our time to be alone and our time to be with others. We will be able to feel how our needs move back and forth, in and out with our own unique rhythm. We can find our own comfort zone when we listen and respect our inner spirit.

Samantha White stayed in a painful marriage far too long. It took her five years to realize she needed to leave. Her bitter, protracted divorce was followed by the death of one of her children and a bout with cancer. After this series of blows, Samantha craved silence and solitude. She found a perfect apartment overlooking the Cape Cod Canal. She walked its shores and collected shells, finding peace and comfort in the gray skies and the cold salty air of winter. It felt like home. It was her sanctuary by the sea.

Samantha stayed connected to a support group of women, driving four hours twice a month to see them. After a year or so she discovered that wasn't enough for her. She began searching for more connections. Her precious solitude turned into loneliness and she finally gave up her perpetual retreat. She rented a room in a private home, with the promise of becoming part of a community. When this didn't work out and the loneliness continued, she decided to move back near Boston. Living alone and being close to her many friends will give her the perfect balance she needs at this time for solitude and community.

There will be periods when we need more time alone, when we need family and friends less. There will be times when our need for solitude is less and we long for more people in our lives. Sometimes we feel sociable and crave parties and crowds while other times one person is one too many.

Nothing stays the same.

We may think something is wrong with us when this change occurs. There is nothing wrong. We change as the tide changes and the sand changes and the weather changes. Some of us need more time to be alone than others. Sometimes five minutes alone can make all the difference in the world. Yet other times we hunger for a ten-day silent retreat.

Is this all part of a larger plan? I don't know for sure, but I think so. I think we are all part of a larger plan and when we honor our need to be alone, we will come closer to knowing how we fit into the ebb and flow of all of life while we are on this earth.

Today I will connect with my own rhythm and honor it whenever possible. ▓

What Is Your "What If?"

I HAVE NOT CEASED BEING FEARFUL, BUT I HAVE CEASED TO LET FEAR CONTROL ME . . . I HAVE GONE AHEAD DESPITE THE POUNDING IN THE HEART THAT SAYS: TURN BACK, TURN BACK, YOU'LL DIE IF YOU VENTURE TOO FAR.

❧ ERICA JONG

Recently I was asked to lead a retreat at a Catholic College. This was not the first time that I would lead a retreat at a religious center and I didn't feel uncomfortable about accepting, even though I am Jewish. The retreats that I lead are spiritual, suitable for anyone and any religion whether the attendees are religious or not.

Both Mass and a time for confessions are scheduled into the Catholic retreats for those who wish to attend. After leading a few similar retreats, I didn't think twice about it. But there was something a little different about this particular one. Before each meal the priest led us in prayer. It seemed to me, all participants crossed themselves first and then recited the prayer with the priest. I bowed my head and joined in the end with amen. At this point I became somewhat uncomfortable.

One of the exercises I had planned to present to the women was something I call "What If?" I offer a series of questions to help uncover where our deepest fears lie and then offer techniques to help them to let go of their fears. One of my deepest fears from childhood is "what will 'they' think of me if they really knew I was Jewish?" I felt that fear beginning to surface, making me very uncomfortable.

When I presented the exercise later, I used my situation as an example. I told them that I was Jewish and my fear was that when they saw I wasn't participating in the prayers they would be sorry they invited me and they certainly wouldn't want me back! When I shared with them there was a murmuring of "It doesn't matter" and "Oh, that's all right!" from the group. I felt better as soon as I told them, no longer carrying something that felt like a secret, a wall between me and the other women. This is exactly how the exercise works. It frees us from our "what ifs."

My old "What will people think?" internalized messages came quite naturally to me. My mother worried so about "what will the neighbors think?" She based many of her life decisions around that fear and never really fulfilled her greatest potential.

For instance, my mother had always told us that my brother and I were second-generation Jews in this country. When she died at the age of 72 years old, I found citizenship papers stating that she had come to this country when she was six years old. I felt confusion at first and then deep sadness for my mother to have carried this secret with her to her grave. I assumed she was trying to protect my brother and me from the anti-Semitism she had experienced when growing up. She must have thought my brother and I would be safer if people thought we were second-generation Jews.

I called my aunt, my mother's older sister by two years, to tell her what I had found. She immediately responded with "Shhh. Promise me you won't tell anyone." While I was filled with great sadness for my aunt, I didn't make that promise because I knew how important it would be for me to share this experience with others.

Some women stay in abusive marriages because their "what if's" are "what if I can't support myself?" and "what if no one else wants me?" and so forth.

Some women won't start their own business because their "what if's" include "What if I fail?"

> Take some time alone to examine your own
> "What if's."
> If you do what you want to do, what is the worst
> that could happen?
> If you say what you want to say, what is the
> worst that could happen?
> If you don't try, how will you ever know?

Today I am examining all my "what if's" and other messages that hold me back. I no longer let my fears of "what if?" keep me from living my life with courage. I can take a chance today and go beyond my comfort zone! ▓

How Important Is It?

I WENT TO THE WOODS BECAUSE I WISHED TO LIVE DELIBER-
ATELY, TO CONFRONT ONLY THE ESSENTIAL FACT OF LIFE,
AND SEE IF I COULD NOT LEARN WHAT IT HAD TO TEACH,
AND NOT, WHEN I CAME TO DIE, DISCOVER THAT I HAD
NOT LIVED.

❧ HENRY DAVID THOREAU, *WALDEN*

The table that was dusted yesterday will need dusting again tomorrow. This will always be so. There will always be more to do. Wherever we turn, we can see something else that needs to be done: a letter to be answered, a weed to be pulled from the garden, a bed to be made, a nose to be wiped, a diaper to be changed, a call to be returned, a bill to be paid.

Our lives can become filled with trivia. We can be caught up in routines until we think they are more important then we are. Routines can run our lives and make our life choices for us. Do the beds really have to be made today? Where did you get that rule? If you went a day or two without making the beds, how many more minutes would you have to relax, not to do some other chore, but to be with yourself.

How much of our rushing and our sense of being over-whelmed is in our heads? How much of it is rooted in patterns that we have played over and over again, that we have told our-selves over and over again until we made them into laws?

My friend Barbara was always rushing. There was never enough time in the day for her. Every time she went by the clock she would say "Oh my God!" One day she received a flash of enlightenment while she was rushing with her 5-year-old son. "Come on, Peter, we have to get going!" He looked at her with the innocent face of a 5-year-old and asked, "Is it time for, 'Oh, my God,' Mommy?" Peter asked.

Children are impressed with the language we use and store it in their memory bank, just as we have been influenced by the language of our own parents. We continue to pass on negative messages to the next generation until we, too, have a flash of enlightenment, slow down our hectic lifestyle, and take time for ourselves.

In her book *The Unknown Woman* Ann Koller writes of a wonderful moment of enlightenment she experienced while taking time in solitude on Nantucket to discover herself. She remembered her mother looking at the clock and gasping. She finally figured out the gasp meant "There won't be enough time." Enough time for her mother meant finishing the housework. Day after day that was what she was about, doing the housework. What is it that your soul needs enough time for?

"Put your ear down next to your soul and listen hard," the poet Anne Sexton tell us. We can't do that in the hectic rush of a normal day. We need quiet. We need solitude. We need to connect with our soul on a daily basis. We need time to make a plan.

Anne Morrow Lindbergh writes that "every person, especially every woman, should be alone sometime during the year, some part of each week, and each day." Why not take the extra minutes that you gained from giving up unnecessary tasks and turn them into alone time for you.

Today I am questioning all the details of my daily life to see what is really important. Today I am finding more time to spend quietly, connecting with my inner spirit. ▓

LOVING
OURSELVES

*WE DO NOT HAVE TO IMPROVE OURSELVES;
WE JUST HAVE TO LET GO OF WHAT BLOCKS
OUR HEART.* ▓

JACK KORNFIELD

Opening Our Hearts

Many years ago I attended a wonderful workshop that changed my life. The workshop was part of a conference at which I was also a presenter. I wish I could remember the workshop leader, so that I could give him proper credit, but I am sorry to say that I can't. The speaker was a dynamic, inspirational minister from California. He led us into a guided imagery to open our hearts.

He suggested we let our hearts stretch to let more love in. The minute he said those words I felt a chill coming over me and I knew I was still blocked. I suddenly felt unworthy of leading my own workshop. I felt unworthy of guiding anyone because I hadn't completed my own work. I hadn't forgiven my own father.

It was not that I had not attempted to forgive him. I had tried to be willing to forgive him a number of times. Every time I thought I was making progress, he would become demanding or angry or sarcastic and I would find myself right back where I started, unable to be in his company without being upset. All my anger from years past would rise within me until I wanted to explode. Here he was, 93 years old, in a nursing home and I was still hoping he would change. Somehow, I had this whole forgiveness thing all wrong.

Today I know that I do not have to be perfect to lead a workshop as long as I am honest. Healing is a process. We make progress through our willingness to let go and let love into our hearts and relationships. Forgiveness is a part of that process. Today I know that forgiveness does not mean we have to accept unhealthy or abusive words or actions. Forgiveness is letting go of, not clinging to, what has been done to us. As Jack Kornfield so simply put it, "If you let go a little, you will have a little peace. If you let go a lot, you will have even more peace."

In solitude, ask yourself questions such as, "What are the things I am holding on to, that are bringing me pain?" "Are there people I have harmed to whom I need to make amends?" "Is there someone I need to forgive?" "Is there a debt I owe or a promise I haven't kept?" "Am I still holding on to anger and resentments?"

I found that by taking time in solitude, I was able to examine what was blocking my heart from feeling love. In doing so I was able to make progress in forgiving and accepting my father. I found that only when we come to the place of love will we find the path to peace in forgiveness we are so desperately seeking.

I will take time to see what is blocking my heart from stretching to let in more love. Then I will practice letting go of it. ▓

What Makes Your Heart Smile?

In a word, what causes the most suffering is your failure to achieve fulfillment, your incompleteness.

▷ MICHEL QUOIST

When we are not being our authentic selves, living a life that is true to our soul, there is a voice within us that sometimes screams and at other times whispers, but it is always there. When we are everyone else's servant, cook, chief bottle washer, nurse, and caretaker, we can pretend not to hear it, but it is always within our hearing. Our creative spirit is always inside, just waiting to be released. When we ignore her, when our innate talent lies dormant, she will never allow us to be satisfied with less than who we are. We can stay very busy and block her out, but deep within we know her truth.

I remember a poem I wrote when I was 17. I was struggling to understand life and my purpose.

> There's something I have to do,
> An urge eating inside of me,
> And until I find out what it is
> I shall never, never be free.
> In the darkness of my thoughts I'm lost,
> I sink within my sins
> In the struggle to know myself
> And just where to begin.

I also remember thinking about that poem again when I was 34, sitting in the office of a psychiatrist. I was in a deep depression, in great emotional and spiritual pain, trying to understand why I couldn't stop drinking and why everything in my life had lost its meaning. A fearful thought haunted me. "Would I be the same at 51?"

Then I remember with great joy driving to work one day when I was 51. The poem I had written at 17 and my deep despair at 34 came back to me and I smiled. I was sober, had turned my life around, and had co-founded a treatment program for women recovering from alcoholism and drug addiction. I knew I was doing what God wanted me to do with my life then. I was listening to my soul.

Author Michel Quoist tells us that what causes us the most suffering is our dissatisfaction, our unrest, our unresolved conflict between what we want and what we actually have, who we would like to be and who we are, our hunger to know the mystery of the world and ourselves. Many of us are doing what we think we should do or what we think other people want us to do.

We don't all have to reach such deep despair, to find out who we really are. Nor can we all simply go off and leave our responsibilities to fulfill our soul's desires, although some women have no choice but to do just that. Perhaps many of us could avoid deep pain and suffering if we follow author Sarah Ban Breathnach's advice. In her wonderful book *Simple Abundance* she suggests: "Maybe if we took an hour a day to paint, to plot, or to throw pots we wouldn't be in pain—physical or psychic."

What voice is calling to you? Is there a talent that you are not expressing? Is there something you liked doing when you were younger that you have not done in a long time? What special dreams have you put off because you are "too busy?" What makes your heart smile?

Today I will take time alone to explore my inner spirit. I will go to that quiet and peaceful place within and ask my wise self if there is something I could be doing to be more authentic. And when I discover what is it, I will make time to include it in my life. ▦

Pressured Solitude

AS A PERSON DEVELOPS HIS OR HER LOVE FOR THE SELF, HE SIMUL-
TANEOUSLY FINDS THE WILL TO DO WHAT IS MOST DIFFICULT.

✤✣ MEISTER ECKHARDT

Nancy, a young woman, recently called me to ask if we had any retreats coming up. She said she just had to get away. Her life was hectic, she had some major decisions to make, and she knew she needed to take some time for herself. "My husband just doesn't understand me. He doesn't understand my need for solitude."

I told her I was in the process of writing a book on Precious Solitude and asked if she would be willing to fill out a questionnaire. I thought it might help her to consider solitude at a deeper level and clarify what it meant in her life.

She misunderstood me and thought I said *"Pressured* Solitude." That really struck a chord with me. Often two things happen for many women. One is that their life is so full of pressure, they feel they have no time for solitude. Second, and simultaneously, many women feel an internal pressure to take time for solitude. This obviously leads to an ongoing conflict. Some women feel the pressure just by thinking of taking the time away from all the things they think they have to do. The thought of all that it takes to even get away for a short while adds even more to the feeling of pressure and can become very overwhelming.

Nancy was also under a great deal of pressure because she wanted her husband to understand and accept her need for solitude. But most of all she wanted his permission. She wanted him to tell her it was okay to take the time because she couldn't tell herself.

I explained to Nancy that all this pressure is put on by ourselves. It's all in our mind. Our thoughts create our pressure. If we think we are so busy we can't get away, we stay in the pressure of everyday life. There is a wonderful line in *Conversations with God* by Neale Donald Walsch: "If you don't go within, you go without." You can choose to continue to have all that pressure by not taking the time to stop. You can continue to go on living without the peace you find when taking the time to go within.

The first pressure, the one that says we don't have enough time and have too much to do is only in our minds. The second pressure, our internal pressure, is really our intuitive self, our inner guide, pressuring us to stop and take time. Even if we think we don't have time to stop, we need to listen to our inner voice. We need to give ourselves permission to follow her if we are to have an authentic life with balance, peace, and spirituality. The only way we can come to peace with both pressures is to listen to and follow this pressure, which comes from within.

When we learn to bring love of ourselves into our lives we discover that we do not need permission from others to take good care of ourselves. As we grow in strength and self-esteem, we honor our own inner guidance. Our own permission is all we need.

When I stop and listen to my inner spirit, I know I am being guided for good and love. Today I am trusting that guidance, knowing I need no other permission than my own to do what is good and right in my life today. ▨

Information Overload

THE BEST THINKING HAS BEEN DONE IN SOLITUDE.
THE WORST HAS BEEN DONE IN TURMOIL.

❧ THOMAS EDISON

We are receiving an incredible amount of information today from a vast number of sources. In addition to everything we've had before, we now have the latest technological development, the "electronic highway" of the Internet and the World Wide

Web. How can we ever keep up? How can we remember everything we think we should remember? How can we remember
what others expect us to remember?

We can't. It's that simple. We just can't. Too much information is coming at us all at once; it's overwhelming.

Sometimes we get so overloaded that we can't even
remember our own telephone number! And there are times
when some of us feel afraid. We wonder if we are losing our
memories or developing Alzheimer's disease. When we are
under stress, the overload feels all the more oppressive.

When precious time alone is a regular part of our daily life,
we can minimize the effects of data overload. We can maintain
a sense of calmness without ever allowing ourselves to become
overly stressed. We stay balanced and centered. It becomes
easier to weed out the important from the trivial. When we
maintain a sense of inner peace and tranquility, outside pressures are less apt to bother us.

This may be an "ideal" because when leading a full and
busy life maintaining inner peace and tranquility at all times is
impossible for most of us. I know of no one who is fully present
in the world who can accomplish this ideal. Even when we are
away from the activities of the world, such as at a retreat or on a
vacation, the bombardment of our own thoughts can disturb
our peace of mind.

When we find ourselves on overload, it's time to take an
important action: withdraw. Even if we have only five minutes,
we need to stop. Change what we're doing. Take a walk.
Meditate. Get away physically, if not mentally. Begin supper. Do
any one of the number of things that are suggested in this book.

*When I find myself stressed and confused I can stop and take some
time for myself. In the quiet time I can give my mind a rest and not
demand from it more than it can handle. I can be gentle with myself.* ▓

Lightening Our Load

*SOLITUDE IS LIKE TAKING A DEEP BREATH
AND ALL THE TENSION GOES OUT OF MY BODY.*

MARCIA LEVY

Imagine that our minds are like filing cabinets. When we are under stress, the filing cabinet slams shut. No matter how hard we try, we cannot open it. All the information we have stored is now unattainable, locked up in that filing cabinet. When we're relaxed, however, the drawers open easily and effortlessly. New information can be stored. Old information can be retrieved.

Sometimes the filing cabinet can become too full to store any more information. We might have to take in less or give our minds a rest. We need to stop taking in any more information and stop struggling to remember what we can't access. When our minds are at rest again, we'll be as sharp as ever!

There are times when I have gone in to the bank to make my deposit and was told I couldn't get a receipt because the computers had shut down. They had received too many data at once and were overloaded.

A dear friend of mine gave me a perfect example of this when she asked me to stop sending her so many e-mail messages. I had a number of people on my e-mail list. When someone forwarded me a good message of inspiration or humor, I would send it to everyone I knew. My friend had spent two weeks on a silent, personal retreat. When she returned, full of peace and clarity, and saw that she had twelve messages from me, the thought of reading them overwhelmed her. She wrote me a very loving note, explaining that this was too much information for her to handle now. She went on to write that she wasn't sure if there would ever be a time when she would be interested in it.

I honored her request right away and took her off my list. This event was immediately followed by a request from someone else, "Thanks for the great e-mails, but since I receive my e-mail at work, the quantity has been a bit overwhelming. Could you please take me off your list?"

Some women do know how to speak up and take care of themselves! In solitude we can ask ourselves:

> Where can I look to lighten my information load?
> Do I have to answer every letter?
> Must I read all the junk mail I receive no matter
>   who sends it?
> Can I ask to be removed from some mailing lists?

By making these and other changes in our lives, we can give ourselves more time to just be in any way we choose.

Today I will take the time to do whatever I need to do to bring peace to the moment. When I feel overwhelmed I will stop and shut out all that is coming at me from my outside world. I will dwell in solitude, even for a few moments, within the peace and quiet of my inside world. ▓

Acceptance

IT IS A STATE OF PEACE TO BE ABLE TO ACCEPT THINGS AS
THEY ARE. THIS IS TO BE AT HOME IN OUR OWN LIVES.

❧ SHARON SALZBERG

If what's going on in our lives is unpleasant, hectic, or unsatisfying, we can obviously see that this is certainly not where we would like to be. Perhaps we're in a job we don't like, but the time isn't right to make a change. Maybe our living arrangement isn't perfect. Maybe a partner has left, or we have to take care of a parent, or we're in a nursing home or even in jail. We are the only ones that can let these things bother us.

Happiness and peace of mind don't have to be dependent on outside conditions. For example, a mother with young children finds less opportunities to take time for herself than someone who is retired. That's just the way it is. Unless you have a great deal of help, you probably have very little time for yourself. This is the simple truth of where you are in your life right now. The more you resist this and resent your reality, the more you suffer.

Perhaps you're older and living in a nursing home, or with a relative, where you must adhere to other people's schedules and rules. You might have more time than you want to yourself. Perhaps there are new situations over which you are powerless, such as your health, or when and what you eat. The more we resist and resent this reality, the more we suffer.

The secret is the same, no matter where we are in our lives. How can we accept that where and what we are doing is exactly where we need to be at this particular time in our lives? By taking our own quiet time, we can build within us the inner serenity that allows us to find a measure of peace, whatever our circumstances.

Is this to say that we will never feel stressed or frazzled or want to scream? Of course not! We are not saints. We are human beings. There are times that are so difficult that the best we can do is to get through them without doing or saying things we will regret later. These times need to be accepted as well. The key here is to accept ourselves as we are in these difficult times. Author Christina Feldman tells us that "Acceptance liberates us to be as we are, and the moment to be as it is" and that "Acceptance increases our capacity to see what is true and live in harmony with this."

We have a tendency to look for blame outside ourselves. "If he weren't so difficult . . . " or "If that hadn't happened . . . " Or "If only I had more money!" In solitude we can learn to accept all things. In these precious, quiet times we can see that all that we think and feel originates from our reaction to what is going on in our lives at that time. Once we gain this wise insight we can help us learn to change our reactions. As corny as the old saying might sound, we can learn to count our blessings, practice gratitude, and accept the chaff and grain alike.

Today, in my quiet time, I will separate the things in my life that I cannot change from the things that I can change. Accepting and letting go of everything on the list of things I cannot change will give me all the energy I need to change what I realistically can. ❧

Making Healthy Decisions

ARE YOU DOING ALL YOU CAN FOR YOUR HEALTH, HAPPI-
NESS, AND POSITIVE FOCUS? ARE YOU DOING IT WITH AN
ATTITUDE OF, "THIS WILL MAKE ME HAPPIER, HEALTHIER AND
MORE POSITIVE . . . ?"

❧ JOHN-ROGER AND PETER McWILLIAMS

Many years ago, in considerable emotional pain, I drove to a retreat center in the mountains. My sole purpose was to seek advice about a major life decision with which I was struggling. Filled with immense anxiety, I stepped out of my car and was met by a friendly looking man whom I had never seen before. "You look sad," he said as he took my hand in welcome. His gentle kindness created such trust in me that I immediately poured out my concerns. I have found his profound wisdom invaluable ever since, not only for myself but also for the many other people with whom I have shared it.

He told me that there are only three ways to make a decision. One is to decide *yes*. One is to decide *no*. And one is to decide *not to decide*. By deciding not to decide, the decision is over for that time. What a relief I felt when I heard that. My tremendous burden was lifted. I didn't need to decide at this time!

He also told me that many of our decisions made today can usually be changed, such as whether or not to take a job, to move, to attend a particular school, or to get married. Just making the decision brings relief.

The word *decide* comes from the Latin word *decidere*. *De* means down, away. *Caedere* means to cut. By deciding yes or no, not today, we are cutting away our burden.

The desire to make the right decision often triggers emotional turmoil. We might be filled with fear or a sense of unworthiness, inadequacy, confusion, or doubt. Leftover feelings from earlier mistakes or times of failure can overwhelm us to the point where we are not able to think at all.

Caroline Myss in her book *The Anatomy of a Spirit* tells us that "how we feel about ourselves, whether we respect ourselves, determines the quality of our life, our capacity to succeed in business, relationships, healing and intuitive skills." She says that self-understanding and acceptance are among the most crucial spiritual challenges we face. "If we do not like ourselves, we will be incapable of making healthy decisions."

Solitude can be helpful and comforting at a time like this. Stepping back, giving ourselves the time and the space to be quiet, removed from interruption, going alone to a quiet place, we can be totally present to what we are feeling. We can watch ourselves go back and forth, being with our confusion, not running away, hiding, or denying it.

It is important that we stay with our feelings. Charlotte Joko Beck tells us that to see how we swing back and forth, when we should stop to just be with our process. "We need to experience the uncomfortableness, the anger, the fear that is sitting beneath the vacillation. Eventually the anger, the upset will begin to shift." Eventually "the barrier of emotion-thought drops and for the first time we can clearly see. When we can, we know what to do. And what we do will be loving and compassionate."

When we don't make a decision, we are actually making a decision not to make a decision! Unless we take the necessary time to think the issue through, other people might make decisions for us or we might lose out on opportunities. When we put off, or don't make a decision, we may be giving up our choice in the matter.

I am learning to trust my intuition. I know that when I turn over my decisions, God gives me the guidance I need. ▓

Solitude in a Crowd

SOLITUDE IS A PRESENCE, NOT AN ABSENCE. SOLITUDE NEVER NEED TO BE DELAYED FOR A MORE CONVENIENT TIME BECAUSE IT RESIDES IN OUR HEARTS AND NOT SIMPLY IN CIRCUMSTANCES.

❧ HUGH PRATHER

There are times when we can be in a crowd of people and yet feel as if we are all alone. Lost within our own minds, we can become oblivious to everyone and everything around us, preferring the company of our own thoughts to conversations with others.

I remember one year. While waiting to have my mammogram, I chatted with the other women waiting with me. It was pleasant and helped to pass the time. The following year felt very different for me. I sat in the same comfortable pleasant waiting room with women I didn't know. This time silence filled the room, broken only by the announcement of someone's name, followed by the rustling of clothes and shuffling of magazines. Someone rose, usually timidly. I could feel the heavy silence following in her wake.

We were all together, joined by our common concerns, and yet, we were each alone. No time for small talk. We were each lost in our own thoughts, fantasies, or prayers; perhaps some of each. This was solitude. Solitude in a room full of people.

"Ruth Fishel?" Hearing my name I stood and followed the voice. It was my turn. I barely spoke to the technician. In other years I was more friendly, asking questions about her job and family. This year she respected my silence. I found a deep sense of peace and comfort being a part of this group of women, each respecting the privacy of each other's thoughts and feelings.

This time I found comfort in knowing I was only one of these women, connected by our sameness, separated by our uniqueness. It was comforting to know there are others who know how I felt. We could choose to reach out and touch someone with our words or remain quiet in our own solitude.

A dear friend recently attended a memorial garden dedication at a school in Sandwich, Massachusetts. Sandwich is a small town on Cape Cod that has, sadly, had more than its share of losses of young people, many due to the terrible combination of driving and alcohol. Dorna had lost an 18-year-old son many years earlier as a result of a motorcycle accident. At this dedication she was in the company of many other parents who had also lost children. "I was, and I expect all of us were, solitary." she told me. "We were all, in a sense, alone with our feelings of grief, anger or hurt or whatever feelings we had and yet, beyond and bigger than that, there was a connectedness we all had with one another."

There are times when we don't have to seek solitude at all but find we are immersed in a very deep place within ourselves. It might feel as if a power beyond ourselves has taken us there for safekeeping. It's important to trust ourselves, letting go of any ways we think we should behave.

Today I am trusting my own instincts, confident that I will know when I need to be alone and when I need to be in the community of others.

Self-Esteem from the Inside Out

WHAT GOES ON IN YOUR INNERMOST BEING IS WORTHY OF YOUR LOVE.

                 RILKE

I have found that each time I do something good for myself, I feel stronger. Each time I take time for myself, I add to my self-esteem. I know it's the right thing to do because it helps me to feel better about myself and more centered. At first, there were times when I felt a bit guilty. "I shouldn't be doing this," I thought, as the old tapes continued to replay. "I should be doing that." "That" being anything on the long list of shoulds that I had assigned to myself or let others assign to me.

As we give ourselves permission to take time for solitude, any guilty feelings about this personal gift recede. Very soon we discover how important it is to our well-being. Very soon we see that we must have this time to feel good about ourselves. Audre Lorde tells us that "caring for myself is not selfish indulgence. It is an act of self-preservation."

Being quiet offers us the opportunity to listen to all the chatter that goes on in our minds. As we learn to become more aware of our old messages, we begin to let them go. We can turn them around to positive and affirming messages, thus continuing to build our personal self-worth. We can take five minutes here, twenty minutes there. And, yes, it makes us feel good. We become aware that we are stronger and more willing to do all the other things that need to be done in the day.

We learn to value ourselves by what we think of ourselves, rather than by what others think of us. The need for other people's approval lessens as our self-approval increases.

Carolyn Myss writes that energy precedes action. The quality of our intention contributes substantially to the results. Therefore simply having the intention to grow, to change, to do good things for ourselves will produce the energy that we need to examine our positive qualities and to strengthen our self-esteem. Inner strength and serenity will grow within us. The better we treat ourselves by giving ourselves the gift of precious time in our day, our week, our month, our lives, the stronger we will be. To cultivate self-respect Christiane Northrop suggests we say this affirmation "I accept myself unconditionally right now."

The Buddha spoke of reflecting on our goodness. It's helpful to take time in solitude and recall any acts of generosity you have performed in your life. Don't look for big things. It can be something as small as stopping to let someone pass in front of you, helping someone out in a time of need, or giving something away to someone who needs it.

Whatever you can remember, recall the good feelings you had at the time you acted generously. Let yourself feel them again. Focus on times such as these rather than on negative things. It will help to strengthen your self-esteem and to feel better about yourself.

Today I know that my need for my own approval is far more important than the approval of others. I will continue to let go of all the self-talk that diminishes me in any way. Today I am my own cheerleader! ▨

Self-Esteem from the Outside In

EVERY POSITIVE CHOICE WE MAKE ENHANCES OUR SELF ESTEEM.

❧ CAROLINE MYSS

When someone tells me I look good or that I've done something well I feel good. When I give someone else a compliment, most often their face lights up and I know I have helped to make them feel good, too.

Self-esteem is a tricky thing. While it's true that it ultimately comes from the inside, it is also reinforced from outside. The more people affirm us, the more we begin to believe in our self-worth.

If people around us treat us as if we have no value, we will begin thinking we have no value. If people around us do not treat us with respect, we will not think we deserve respect and will not expect to be treated with respect.

Years ago I read *I Ain't Much, Baby, But I'm All I Got* by Jess Lair. He described how he changed his life after suffering from a life-threatening illness. He realized that his time was very limited, so he chose to spend time only with the people who made him feel "ten feet tall!" It's a wonderful premise for deciding whom to spend our time with.

When we were younger, we did not have the power to make such choices. Negative messages were given to us by people who didn't value us as we deserved to be valued or by people who wanted to change us. Today we can choose to be in the company of people who mirror back the growing, positive self-esteem that we find in solitude. We can choose to be with people who respect our need for solitude.

In quiet time we can examine the people in our lives and see if they are positive and supporting. We can ask ourselves if our friends make us feel "ten feet tall."

I will do everything I can to surround myself with positive people. I choose to be friends with people who are on a spiritual path and support me in my growth. 🏵

Honoring Our Own Special Time

WHAT A COMMENTARY ON OUR CIVILIZATION, WHEN BEING ALONE IS CONSIDERED SUSPECT; WHEN ONE HAS TO APOL-OGIZE FOR IT, MAKE EXCUSES, HIDE THE FACT THAT ONE PRACTICES IT—LIKE A SECRET VICE.

❧ ANNE MORROW LINDBERGH

Years ago I made a commitment to myself that I would medi-tate daily. Whether I was at home or away, I didn't change my morning ritual. From years of struggle with self-discipline, I knew that if I missed one day it would be easy to skip two days and then three days. Then it would be difficult to get back into my routine again.

My usual routine in those days was to go to the kitchen for a cup of coffee and then go back to my bedroom, where I would read something inspirational, meditate, and then pray. (It's still the same without the coffee.) I was surprised to find that when other people were present, such as when I had weekend guests or when I stayed at someone else's home, I was very uncomfort-able. If someone was in the kitchen, that person would usually begin a conversation. I felt as if I was being rude by excusing myself to meditate, but I forced myself to do it anyway.

The same held true if I wanted to go for a walk. I thought I was being rude and selfish to take this time for myself—alone time which I craved. But again, it was so necessary for my well-being that I went beyond my discomfort and excused myself. I was often flooded with thoughts such as "I hope they won't think I'm rude. I hope they'll still like me." These were old messages born of childhood insecurity and self-doubt.

As time passed, it became easier and more natural for me to take time for myself. Now friends and family take it for granted that I always take time in solitude to meditate or take walks alone. There have been precious times when I knew grandchildren were peeking into my room to see what it looks like when Gramma Ruth is meditating. I smile inside without changing the expression on my face. It's good for them to know it's okay to take time for yourself. It's good for them to learn to respect someone else's time for solitude.

Some women told me they feel so awkward in front of a roommate, partner, or spouse that they would only meditate when they were alone in their homes. A few others said that they were embarrassed because they were told that meditation is foolish and a waste of time. How sad! How else can we know who we are if we don't take time alone? How else can we honor our uniqueness, connect with our inner spirit, and nurture our soul? How else can we grow into interdependent, strong spiritual women if we let our fears and insecurities block us from our time of communication with our Higher Power. Bellyclare Moffatt writes, "When you consistently enter the silence . . . you will come to a place (it is different for each of us and yet it is the same) where there is nothing. Nothing at all." She calls this the Listening Soul.

I value my special time alone and will not let anyone interfere with it. It is important that I move beyond any feelings of insecurity or self-doubt. My time in silence and solitude is essential to being a complete woman. ✼

Honoring Our Own Needs

In solitude I can unclench my jaws, stomach and adrenalin. I can be me—often indolent and self-absorbed, but also content and thankful for the small happy joys—reading, eating ice cream and cuddling the cat.

❧ Marie Stilkind

Emily, our cat, knows just what she needs and she honors it. She takes care of herself. When she wants to be petted, she moves close. She purrs when she is petted just the way she likes it best, and when she's had enough she moves away. If she doesn't want to be touched, no amount of begging, bribing, or cajoling will change her mind.

When she is in the mood, Emily retires to a distant chair or stretches out on the floor where I'm sure she thinks the rays of the sun are here on this earth for the sole purpose of keeping her warm. When the weather is warm, she lies by the back screen door and lets the breeze keep her cool.

Emily didn't have to read books on how to take better care of herself or go to workshops or be in therapy. She just does what comes naturally. She moves toward or away from people and situations according to her moods. She follows her inner knowing.

When the grandchildren visit, Emily first sits in a distant chair or under the dining room table so she can observe them. "Are they going to be rough or gentle? Will they chase me and pull my tail or will they leave me alone?" she seems to be thinking. Experience has taught her that as much as they want to be gentle, their petting can be a bit rough. So it's her habit to retreat after a time to a safe place until they leave. Noise bothers Emily and young children are naturally noisy. They run and they yell and they're uninhibited. They have fun!

The grandchildren appreciate their own space, as well. When they're tired of being with the adults, they'll simply go off into the bedroom and play with the toys there. They don't even ask permission or excuse themselves for being rude. They, like Emily, move in their own time and pace.

If taking care of themselves comes so naturally to cats and small children, why doesn't it come so naturally to us? Well, for one thing, we've been told that it's selfish to place ourselves first. We've been taught to be polite. We've been "socialized," which often means putting everyone else before ourselves. And we often care too much about what other people think of us.

We need to retrain ourselves and give ourselves permission to move at our own time and pace, too. We can learn that it's okay to excuse ourselves from company when we want some time to ourselves. For many of us, life has brought us to an absence of self-awareness. We no longer respond to our inner prodding for time alone or quiet time! Like Emily, we need to sit back on a distant chair and observe our own needs.

I am learning more and more to trust my own wisdom and give myself permission to follow it. ✺

Beginning Our Day with Love

WAKING FROM SLEEP IS AWAKENING. WAKING UP FROM IGNORANCE IS ENLIGHTENMENT. ENLIGHTENED PEOPLE ARE THOSE WHO HAVE AWARENESS IN LIFE, WHO ARE FREE FROM PSYCHOLOGICAL SLEEP, WHATEVER THEY ARE DOING.

❧ DHIRAVAMSA

There is a very soft and gentle moment between sleep and waking. In this moment there are no thoughts. In this moment we really do experience nothing but the present moment. We gradually become aware and then . . . BOOM! Thoughts begin pouring into our mind, disturbing this beautiful, peaceful state. Depending on where we are emotionally and spiritually, our body begins to respond to our thoughts.

Our bodies do not know the difference between something real or something imagined. They will react the exact same way in each situation. For example, if you woke up thinking of something you were looking forward to in the upcoming day, your first awareness would be one of pleasure and your body would react and be relaxed. On the other hand if your first thoughts were of four interviews for a new job and you forgot to set the alarm and you overslept, your body would be tense and you would immediately feel stress. Everything you felt was only set off by a thought.

Take some time for yourself before you get out of bed, even if it is only a few minutes. If you are late for an appointment, it's still better in the long run to take these few minutes for yourself. You'll bring a sense of peace and confidence with you, which will be far more effective than rushing in, feeling scattered and upset.

As you become aware of being awake, gently notice whatever thoughts are going through your mind. Notice your reactions to your thoughts. Be with your reactions. Let everything be just as it is and notice the feelings as they pass by. Breathe in gently and say quietly to yourself, "Good morning!" Know that every time you breathe in gently, you are releasing your endorphins, your body's natural "feel good" chemicals. Feel peace and well-being flowing through your body with every in-breath. Feel tension, concerns, or fears leave your body with every out-breath.

Know that you are now being filled with positive, loving, and healing energy. Know that you will be carrying this energy with you throughout your day. Know that you can connect with this energy again and again throughout the day.

Here is one of my favorite prayers for starting the day off in a good mood:

So far today, God, I've done all right. I haven't gossiped, haven't lost my temper, haven't been greedy or grumpy, nasty, or self-centered. I'm really glad about that. But in a few minutes, God, I'm going to get out of bed, and then I'm going to need a lot of help. Thank you.

Take this peaceful time in solitude to say your own morning prayer, asking for guidance during the day. If you have any concerns for yourself or others, turn them over to your Higher Power.

In this wonderful place between sleep and consciousness, no one has to even know that we are awake. We can keep our eyes closed, stay still, and greet the day in our own special way.

I begin my day with quiet time, finding peace and serenity to carry with me for the rest of the day. As I lie quietly connecting with God, I know I can handle anything that comes up today. ▓

Passing On the Gift of Solitude

SOLITUDE CAN BE YOUR MOST MEANINGFUL COMPANION AND IT CAN ASSIST YOU IN BEING A MORE GIVING PERSON IN YOUR SPIRITUAL PARTNERSHIPS. RATHER THAN REGARDING YOUR PARTNER'S NEED FOR TIME ALONE AS A THREAT, SEE IT AS A TIME OF RENEWAL THAT YOU CELEBRATE. MAKE EVERY EFFORT TO HELP EACH OTHER HAVE THAT SPACE. TREAT THAT SPACE AS SACRED.

❧ WAYNE DYER

Kerrie, one of my clients, felt very threatened when her fiancee wanted time to be by himself. He suffers from carpel tunnel syndrome from years of working with computers and there are times when his pain is so severe that all he wants to do is to lie down and wait for it to pass. Kerrie felt abandoned, a feeling left over from her childhood. As much as her fiancee reassured her that he loved her and was not leaving her, she still felt shut out and lonely every time he needed his time alone. She felt compelled to go into the bedroom and make sure he loved her. It took great effort for her to be able to leave his door closed and busy herself in meditation or a book.

Our children need their own time, too. We don't have to rush to rescue a child every time he or she complains of boredom. If we give them too much attention, they will become dependent adults and never learn the value of amusing themselves or the gift of being alone with themselves.

What better gift can we give someone else than something we value ourselves? We can give a neighbor or a daughter the gift of babysitting, so they can take time for solitude. We can be generous with our partner or spouse, our friends and colleagues, and not demand too much of their time and attention. We want others to be sensitive to us and respect our need for solitude. We can repay that gift by passing it on. Part of loving ourselves is to know we are capable of passing that love on to others.

I am learning to be sensitive to the needs of the people in my life and can find ways to make their time for solitude possible. ✴

A TIME
TO HEAL

*ONLY INTIMACY WITH THE SELF WILL
BRING ABOUT TRUE HEALING.* ✸

DEEPAK CHOPRA

Through the Tough Times

OUR QUESTION WILL NOT BE JOB'S QUESTION "GOD, WHY ARE YOU DOING THIS TO ME?" BUT RATHER "GOD, SEE WHAT IS HAPPENING TO ME. CAN YOU HELP ME?" WE WILL TURN TO GOD NOT TO BE JUDGED OR FORGIVEN, NOT TO BE REWARDED OR PUNISHED, BUT TO BE STRENGTHENED AND COMFORTED.

✣ RABBI HAROLD S. KUSHNER

On the morning of October 12, 1992, my 29-year-old son, Bob, called from Pittsburgh, where he was attending graduate school. He was in great emotional pain, under tremendous stress. We talked for forty-five minutes. I suggested he pray and he did, while we were still on the phone. He turned over his fears and concerns to God. I felt strength coming from him through the telephone wires before we hung up and I thought he was all right. Later that afternoon, in spite of our talk and his prayers, Bob's pain overpowered him again and he chose to end his life.

Through all that followed I felt God with me. I can't describe it exactly, but I had the feeling I was wrapped in a cocoon of love. My pain was so deep it was beyond description. I knew I was being guided each step along the way through the devastating days that followed. Often I felt I wasn't breathing, just going through the motions of living.

There were times afterward when I found myself worrying that in a moment of insanity I might even take my own life. On the day of his funeral I looked out of my bedroom window and saw the beautiful October foliage. I remember thinking "Bob will never see this again! How could he make such a choice?" At that moment I knew I would be all right. I felt a deeper sense of the beauty of the universe than I had ever experienced before and knew I wanted to continue to experience it and live. I knew God was part of everything.

I also knew God had no part in Bob's death. I surprised myself for not thinking, "If there is a God, how could He or She let this happen to Bob?" I knew that Bob had a choice. His choice was to become free of pain in the only way he knew in that instant.

I spent long periods alone after this happened. Even when I was with people I often felt alone. Writing was a great release for me. For almost a full year I wrote and wrote and wrote. My computer is full of all my feelings and thoughts. What I couldn't express verbally I did express with my writing.

Two years later I went away by myself for a few days, parking our twenty-seven-foot recreational vehicle at a quiet and peaceful camp site. I reflected on all the years of Bob's life and my relationship with him. Through prayer, meditation, and writing I was able to let go of any guilt and blame I held in my heart. I forgave myself for not being a perfect mom.

Personal retreats can be a great comfort in times of pain and loss. Going off by myself in our RV was perfect for me. A retreat house, a monastery, or a cabin by the lake might be more suitable for you.

The only caution is that we have to be sure that we are ready for the solitude. It took me two years to take this time to be alone by myself. Then one day I just knew it was the right time. I realized I was strong enough to look deeply into my heart and soul and release any self-blame I still carried. I found things happen in God's time, not ours. We need to trust our inner guidance to know the right time.

I trust and follow my inner guidance today. The universe provides me with all that I need to do what is good and right for me. 🕮

Reaching Wellness through Solitude

MYSTICS REPORT THAT EVERY BIT OF THE WORLD RADIATES FROM ONE CENTER—EVERY CRICKET, EVERY GRAIN OF DUST, EVERY DREAM, EVERY IMAGE, EVERYTHING UNDER THE SUN OR BEYOND THE SUN, ALL ART AND MYTH AND WILDNESS. IF THEY ARE RIGHT, THEN WE HAVE NO MORE IMPORTANT TASK THAN TO SEEK THAT CENTER.

❧ SCOTT RUSSELL SANDERS

Jeanne Jackson, a nurse healer, had a chronic neck pain as a result of an automobile accident. At one time it became so debilitating that she couldn't work and went into a multi-dimensional crisis: spiritual, emotional, and physical. Her life broke down so badly that she had to go inside to the deepest, darkest place of her pain to find insights into what was going on in her life that could have caused such a breakdown.

As she dared to look deeper and deeper into her past, she could see all the armor she had created to protect herself from psychic pain. Gradually she began to remember what she had been blocking all her life—that she had been sexually abused as a child.

In solitude Jeanne was able to make contact with the way she had protected and isolated herself because she had felt so threatened, ashamed, and helpless deep into her core self. She worked on this alone in solitude and with other healers and therapists.

Now Jeanne thinks of solitude as peaceful aloneness. She says "It's time to be with me and come to know me. It's time to see what I'm thinking and feeling." She now practices Chi

Gong, an energy exchange, every morning as part of her spiritual ritual. Jeanne says it connects her to the universe and she feels centered, awake, alert, peaceful, connected. After sitting with those feelings for ten or fifteen minutes, she feels better and has more energy to help herself and others.

Jeanne's deep pain helped her to search for what she calls her soul's journey. She saw that she had to heal from her past so that she could do what she was placed on this earth to do . . . serve humankind.

Jan spends twelve hours a week on kidney dialysis. Because of her experience with solitude she has been able to cope with this difficult situation and feel comfortable with herself.

Dr. Kathryn L. Haycock told me, "Rediscovering the beauty and peace of solitude has been one of the greatest gifts of my diagnosis with breast cancer. Solitude means a chance to connect with my center, my source, who I truly am and who I am capable of being." She has gone through a very difficult time, with many flare-ups. After each flare-up she would spend one or two hours alone in bed, working on her feelings and the thought processes around them, regaining perspective and focus and she has been responding well to treatments.

Rhonda is also healing from breast cancer. After her chemotherapy she went for a walk. She prayed and said, "I'm afraid." The message came back: "I am with you. Everything will be all right." Rhonda said it felt like a warm, reassuring embrace from the universe. She cried tears of gratitude.

Retired editor Marie Stilkind became very ill once. She hardly dared to go out. When she returned home from simple errands such as grocery shopping, she collapsed onto her bed. She didn't even have enough energy to pray. "Without my solitude," she said, "my time to recuperate, I would not have survived."

It is wonderful to know that extended quiet time in solitude, whether it be in prayer, meditation, or contemplation, is always there when healing is needed. ✠

Special Times for Healing

ALL PROBLEMS FADE OUT IN PROPORTION AS YOU DEVELOPE
THIS ABILITY TO BE QUIET, TO BEHOLD AND TO WITNESS
DEVINE HARMONY UNFOLD.

✠ JOEL GOLDSMITH

Our need for solitude varies. Some women spend some period of time alone as part of their daily routine. These times often lengthen when challenging times occur. Some women rarely think of solitude except when difficult times come up, and then they turn to it for comfort and healing. Many women have experienced critical times in their lives, which solitude has helped make bearable.

Jean shared with me that when her son was heavily into drugs, she needed time alone for meditation and prayer so that she could trust that she would be able to handle anything that would happen.

When Toby Kalman's daughter died she felt she needed to continue her work. Her heart was broken. She was fortunate enough to have friends who were bird watchers who taught her of a special place. "Early in the mornings, before daylight, I watched these small miracles awaken. I learned their sounds, their silhouettes, their patterns through my many tears. I pretty much washed myself out in my private times so I could be present at work."

Genevieve grew up in an abusive family. "I would take our dog for long walks to a scraggly beach about two miles from our home. He and I would prowl the beach, looking for smooth and pretty rocks, he'd sit with me on the beach staring at the passing ships or at the waves, or we'd walk as far as we could up and down the beach. Often we were the only ones there. Looking at the lake helped me put myself and my problems into some kind of perspective. They were really pretty small compared to the lake, let alone the world. The sound of the waves, the smell, the search for rocks, all while alone with my dog, helped me gain strength to go back to the house. I used those times alone to regroup, look to the future, and hope for better times."

As a new mother, Barbara realizes solitude is one of the things that was left by the wayside when her baby was born and that it might be part of the reason she felt so confused and unsure of many things. "Without time for reflection I find myself responding to life reflexively and getting caught up in the details; feeling like a hamster on a wheel, forever running just to maintain."

One woman told me that when she became sober she needed the time to work just on herself and had to forget the needs of her family. And another woman shared that she needed solitude to stop lying to herself and take a good look at her life, so she could stay sober or there would be nothing left for her family.

Sad times such as sickness, death, and anniversaries of deaths, divorces, and separations all are listed as times when solitude has been important. Another woman told me her entire family of origin had died, one at a time and she required extra quiet and peace at the ocean during those times. Another time she was living overseas and some days felt very foreign and hard. She relished closing the doors, eating peanut butter toast, and reading by the fire. It restored her energy.

It is comforting to know that the special peace we find in solitude, when we can connect with our inner world and the God of our understanding is always there for us, whatever we are going through.

Today I have all the faith and trust I need to know that whatever happens, I am always okay. I simply need to spend time in solitude connecting with all the healing energy the universe provides. ▓

Letting Go

ALL THE FLOWER KNOWS HOW TO DO IS BLOOM.

☘ JEANIE MARSHALL

I was startled one day by an unusually loud noise at my bird feeder. It was a huge black starling, the first I had ever seen at the feeder. Afraid that the starling would scare away the small song birds, I was about to clap my hands and make loud noises, Instead, I just stopped, took a long deep breath, and walked slowly back to my desk.

I remembered the time when I had a major war with squirrels a few years earlier when I had put up a new bird feeder. Every time I filled the feeder, squirrels would greedily eat up most of the seeds. I tried putting up one barrier after another to dissuade the squirrels. It was all to no avail. With each new barrier, the squirrels would try to climb to the feeder, fail to get there, and then leave. I was left with the confidence that I had won! But then, within minutes, another squirrel arrived, swishing his tail, and pacing back and forth, looking over the situation. He eventually found a way to reach the feeder.

I finally learned my lesson when I greased the post with cooking oil. I imagined the squirrel would feel the oil and give up. I never anticipated their tenacity would push them to attempt the climb. I watched with horror as a squirrel slipped on the oil and fell ten to fifteen feet to the ground. Not daring to see what happened to the squirrel, I asked a friend to check and see if the squirrel was dead. With much trepidation, she went to look. Much to my relief, she could not find the squirrel. Somehow it had survived the fall, picked itself up, and had run away. I marveled at the squirrel's creativity, admiring his stubbornness, resilience, and fortitude.

Finally, I invested $8.95 in a real squirrel shield. I was pleased by their very existence. I was not the only neurotic bird fancier. If such shields were manufactured, other people must share my frustrations as well. When the squirrels saw this new shield, they paced back and forth, looked quizzically up and down and around and finally left. Now they come back occasionally, make a screaming angry sound, swoosh their tails, and finally leave.

I had beaten the squirrels, but I beat myself as well. I could no longer watch the birds from my desk because the shield made the feeder hang lower on the tree branch.

Here I was, in a near-battle mode again, over a starling. Was I willing to go through all that again? I could feel my own tension growing as I, like the squirrels, began to pace back and forth trying to figure it out. Is this how I wanted to feel? How important was this? And why did I even want the little song birds to be able to have access to the feeder, rather than this large starling?

The squirrels were incredibly inventive. They simply wanted the food. The starlings simply wanted the food. My job was to let go and let nature take its course.

Animals and birds go where their instincts take them. My pride and my ego had been driving me. I became willing at last to stop trying to change them.

How many times do we try make something happen that just doesn't work? How often do we think that if we try this or that, the results will be better?

Letting go is one of the most freeing choices we have. Trying the best we can, then leaving the results to God or nature is one way to release our frustrations. Peace comes when we become willing to accept reality as it is.

As you take time for solitude today, you might want to consider what you are holding on to. Have you been trying to change something for a long time and it just doesn't happen? Is there something you have been hanging on to that has been causing you a lot of pain? Whenever you are ready for these questions, your life will begin to open in ways that you cannot imagine. Being willing is all that it takes to start.

I am willing to begin to look deeper into the places that keep me stuck. I am becoming willing to look, to see, to accept, and to let go. ▓

Face to Face with Ourselves

SO SOLITUDE, THAT CRUCIBLE IN WHICH THE HEART IS PURIFIED AND CLEANSED . . . IS A PLACE OF GRACE . . . WHERE THE SPIRIT WORKS GRADUALLY BUT SURELY TO RENEW THE SELF.

❧ BURTON CHRISTIE

I'll never forget the shock I felt the first few times I consciously came face to face with myself. Early in my recovery from alcoholism, a friend was helping me get in touch with my feelings. She asked me to list the five things I most disliked about my husband. That was easy and I listed them quickly. She then asked if I had any of those characteristics. "Definitely not!" I remember exclaiming. She asked me to look again. "Well, maybe a little of this. And just maybe a little of that." "Look again," she pushed. I remember feeling the heat of embarrassment sweep over me. I am olive complexioned and rarely blush, but I felt I was blushing then. I saw what I didn't want to see. I, too, to some degree, possessed all those traits I so disliked in my husband. It was a rare time for me and the beginning of a path of self-searching and taking personal responsibility for my life and my happiness.

As my awareness grew I saw that I had no idea who I really was without alcohol in my system. I needed more time by myself for deeper exploration.

I saw how I always blamed people and situations for my unhappiness. It took time for me to learn that it wasn't the *hims* or *hers*, or the *this's* or *that's*. The answer lay within me and only I had the power to change me. It was exciting and promising and exhilarating and scary! It wasn't easy.

There are times when we can't wait to get away. Perhaps we are going to a retreat or an afternoon hike. Instead of the peace we expected, the peace we so desperately desired, ghosts from the past come in and join us. Guilt and shame over the past mistakes and fear of the unknown future can overwhelm us. Face to face with ourselves we can see that we haven't changed. Just the scenery around us has changed.

Alone we can find that coming face to face with ourselves is a gift. By allowing ourselves to be with whatever comes up in each moment, we make it possible to know ourselves at a much deeper level. All that comes up has always been there. It has simply been drowned out or covered over by our various modes of denial and self-protection, such as too much working, television, food, alcohol, drugs, gambling, thrill-seeking, or any other way we habitually block self-knowledge.

Take some time in solitude and to achieve a deeper understanding of yourself. Perhaps you can think of someone you don't care for and list five reasons why. Then honestly explore whether you have some of those same characteristics.

Now list five characteristics of someone you admire. Then honestly explore whether you have those characteristics as well. Often the people we admire touch something within us that we share, too.

Today I have the faith and courage to seek a deeper understanding of myself. In solitude I can be free to be completely who I am, looking at all sides of me with love and acceptance. ▓

Letting the Tears Flow

LET YOUR TEARS COME. LET THEM WATER YOUR SOUL.

❧ EILEEN MAYHEW

In the best of times, life brings us great joy; and in the worst of times, great pain. For the most part, we live somewhere in between, experiencing mild ups and downs. Most of us have no problem with the ups and even the downs when they are mild and certainly not the times of great joy. Frequently, as much as we wish it weren't the case, life is out of our control. When sadness, fear, disappointments, and losses find their way into our lives, many of us have difficulty coping.

Many of us were taught to "keep a stiff upper lip" or "keep our troubles to ourselves or within our own homes." Some women turn to doctors or psychiatrists for pills to "get through their pain." Neither way works in the long run. When I went to a psychiatrist for help with my drinking problem way back in 1971, he said, and I will never forget his words, "There, there, dear, you're just a little neurotic. With a few pills and a few visits, you'll be just fine." Unfortunately, women are often still treated the same way. "Just take a few pills. . . . "

As hard as it might be, we have to feel our feelings before they can leave us. When we stuff them, keep a stiff upper lip, or anesthetize them with alcohol, drugs, or prescription pills we might think we're keeping them in control. But at best, we receive only temporary relief. We are doing more damage to ourselves than we realize. Golda Meir said "Those who do not know how to weep with their whole heart don't know how to laugh either." When we don't allow ourselves to feel our pain, have our pain, and express our pain, we block ourselves from feeling love and joy.

When we allow ourselves to have our feelings, we will discover that we can handle them. We will realize they will not destroy us or make us fall apart. By just being ourselves with whatever is going on in the present moment, our pain becomes fluid. As we open to being with it, it softens and we become softer and less fearful. We're able to handle more and more of the pain and we see that it often comes in waves and then passes on. It is true that some losses can cause pain that can last a lifetime, but it becomes a less powerful presence in our lives, as long as we let ourselves feel it. There's a wonderful Indian proverb that tells us "The soul would have no rainbow if the eyes had no tears."

Sometimes work, family, and activities may keep you from feeling your feelings. Be gentle with yourself. Take time for yourself. Take time in solitude to feel your feelings and let the tears flow. Someone once said that tears are God's way of washing away our pain.

I allow myself to feel all my feelings, even the ones I don't want to feel. I can laugh as well as cry today, holding nothing back. I know I am safe in each moment. ✠

The Burdens of the Past

WHEN THE SHADOW IS EMBRACED, IT CAN BE HEALED.
WHEN IT IS HEALED, IT TURNS INTO LOVE.

❧ DEEPAK CHOPRA

At a conference many years ago, I watched author and lecturer Robert Ackerman dramatize very graphically what it looked like to carry our past with us. He walked across the stage, hunched over with the burden of the heavy sack he was carrying over his shoulder.

"What's in your sack?" someone asked.

"My mother," he answered.

"Isn't she heavy?"

"She sure is!"

"Why don't you put her down?"

"I can't."

"Well, why can't you stop carrying her?"

"I don't know. I've always carried her."

We could see clearly how it is such a waste of time and energy to carry the heavy burdens of the past with us. Shame and guilt destroy our present moment. Resentments make healthy relationships impossible.

Some women fear solitude because of what might come up that still causes them pain. But whatever we choose not to look at stays stuck within us and eventually wears down our immune systems, weakening it until we become physically ill.

Taking special time alone for the sole purpose of examining all the things we still carry in our bag is time well spent. And we don't need to take out everything at once.

There's a wonderful story about a woman who always cuts a few inches from her pot roast before she puts it into the pan to cook. One day her daughter asked her why she does this. "I don't know," she answered. "My mother always did it that way." Not willing to stop there, the daughter went to her grandmother and asked the same question. "I don't know," answered her grandmother. "My mother always did it that way." Still not willing to take this for the finally reason, and fortunate to have her great grandmother still living, she paid another visit with the same question. "Because the pot is too small!" answered her great grandmother.

How often do we stay in ruts, stuck in old, obsolete ways of doing things? What do we still hold on to that we have outgrown? What are we clinging to because we are afraid to let it go? In solitude we can take out our pen and paper and examine our patterns and habits that no longer serve us in a healthy way.

It is said that God never gives us more than we can handle. When memories come up we can choose to push them away by getting busy, but they don't really completely go away. They will be back to haunt us until we are willing to stop and let them surface and deal with them.

Writing is a very helpful technique to explore our past. In a notebook or journal you can ask yourself questions such as:

What events and situations still bother me?

Am I still carrying guilt and shame?

Know that the purpose for asking these questions is to let go of the past. Expressing the concerns on paper and becoming willing to let them go is a beginning. Later, it's good to talk things over with a friend or a sponsor. If situations continue to bother us, a good therapist or counselor can helps us work things through.

Today I am willing to do whatever I can to let go of all situations and patterns in my past that keep me locked in yesterday. I am not letting memories block me from discovering the joys of solitude and the pleasure of simply being with myself. ▨

Forgiveness

WE ACHIEVE INNER HEALTH ONLY THROUGH FORGIVE-
NESS—THE FORGIVENESS NOT ONLY OF OTHERS BUT ALSO
OF OURSELVES.

❧ RABBI JOSHUA LOTH LEIBMAN

Many years ago I was involved with creating a greeting card line for our alcoholism treatment program. Its combined purpose was to raise money for our program and give the women in it an opportunity for job training. It took many months to get it off the ground. Just when it looked like it was on the verge of becoming successful, our artist came to me without any warning and said, "Ruth, I am leaving this week and I don't want to discuss it." Then, she stalked out of the room.

I was stunned, furious, confused, and disappointed. How could she do this to us! *A Course in Miracles* tells us that we are either coming from a place of love or a place of fear. The Course's aim is to remove the blocks to the awareness of love's presence. The book states, "All healing is essentially the release from fear." I knew I was in a place of fear; afraid that we would lose this business we were building, afraid that I wouldn't find another artist as good. I spent time alone meditating and praying to be able to say something positive and loving, to have the grace to come from a place of love rather than this place of fear I was in.

A few days later I was able to go to her and tell her how sad I was that she was leaving and how much I would miss her without expressing my anger and fear. As soon as those words came out of my mouth, the tightness around my heart lifted and I was able to feel love for her again. She burst into tears and we hugged each other. "I was so afraid you would be angry at me!" she said. "I need to go home to my family. I'm so sorry I am leaving you now."

Author and co-founder of Spirit Rock Meditation Center Jack Kornfield writes, "Forgiveness is an act of the heart, a movement to let go of pain . . . a way of softening the heart and releasing the barriers to our loving kindness and compassion. It does not mean to justify or condone. It is just letting go of the burden." He suggests that we sit quietly and let ourselves feel the barrier that we have been holding on to and that has kept our heart from opening.

Spiritual leaders throughout time have taught us that we must forgive ourselves and others. From our sudden loss of our artist, I came to understand the words of Reinhold Niebuhr when he said "Forgiveness is the final form of love." We have to forgive ourselves for all the ways, knowingly or not, that we have harmed, betrayed, and abandoned ourselves and others. And we have to ask for forgiveness from those we have harmed.

Forgiveness opens our hearts so that we may be able to feel love. Take time in solitude so see if there is any unfinished business in your life. Ask yourself:

Is there someone I need to forgive or receive forgiveness from?

Is there someone I need to make amends to?

I am willing to release all the resentments on to which I have been holding. I am willing to forgive myself. I am willing to ask forgiveness to those I have harmed. I am willing to do all this so I can be free to love myself and others. ▩

Enjoying Our Own Company

WHEN WE CANNOT BEAR TO BE ALONE, IT MEANS WE DO
NOT PROPERLY VALUE THE ONLY COMPANION WE WILL HAVE
FROM BIRTH TO DEATH—OURSELVES

❧ EDA LeSHAN

Author Anne Harmon spent a great deal of time alone as a child. Her parents were busy and felt that since her grandmother lived downstairs, Anne would be fine. Once a man in the neighborhood who was a deaf mute and who smelled of alcohol, entered the house looking for Anne's father. He walked through all the rooms, including Anne's bedroom, and left when he couldn't find him. Anne was terrified by the experience and, as a consequence, she developed an extraordinary fear of being alone. Panic attacks became common. Sometimes she had to pull her car over to the side of the road to wait for an anxiety attack to pass.

Years later Anne and her husband bought a piece of land in Vermont, where they spent many happy weekends together. Her husband encouraged her to stay behind when he returned to his job during the week. The thought of being alone was so disturbing that Anne was not able to even try it until the year she turned sixty. Until that time, whenever she did stay in Vermont without her husband, at least one of her children or grandchildren stayed with her.

One winter day while driving Anne skidded on ice, crashed, and completely totaled her car. In a flash she wondered whether she was going to die, but in that same instant she experienced a spiritual awakening. In that second she knew that she was being taken care of and that whatever happened, she would be all right. She knew she was no longer only a physical being but a spiritual being as well.

Still, the first time she dared to be alone she was terrified. She had her dog with her for comfort and knew she could call her daughter if it became too difficult. By the evening she began to feel comfortable and soon she was amazed to find she felt wonderful.

In years past, when she wanted to escape from whatever was going on, she would disappear into a book. Now Anne enjoys the beauty of the mountains, sky, and flowers. Anne now feels so much more spiritual when she is by herself. She talks to Mother Earth and the trees and gets answers she never thought possible. When deeply troubled by something that might be going on with her children she hears the message "Let go of this" in her mind. Today she can do that.

I, too, have had difficulty with prolonged silence. My very first silent retreat lasted two days. It was years more before I dared experience a three-day silent retreat and many more years until I could try a seven-day silent retreat. How could I possibly get through so much time alone? I feared experiencing either boredom or insanity! Now I know that there is nothing to be feared in time alone. Only my own thoughts can disturb my peace of mind. And I know today that since I create my own thoughts, I can change or stay with them. That is my choice.

Making friends with solitude can begin at any age. We can begin with a few minutes here and a few minutes there, building our confidence into a faith that can sustain us through hours and then days. If painful memories appear we can tell ourselves that those are not real today. They are just memories, part of our past. If uncomfortable feelings arise, we can write them down or talk about them to a tape recorder. This releases their power over us and saves them for a later time when we can talk them over with a friend or a therapist.

Know that we are never truly alone. Connecting with nature can anchor us. Connecting with our Higher Self through prayer and meditation can soothe our difficult moments.

I do not have to let any fears of being alone stop me from discovering the joys of solitude. 🎐

When Solitude Is Not a Choice

WHAT A LOVELY SURPRISE TO DISCOVER HOW UNLONELY BEING ALONE CAN BE.

ELLEN BURSTYN

Diane Shrank is a remarkable 42-year-old woman, a holistic counselor, writer, and former attorney, whose body is significantly disabled from multiple sclerosis. She says, "I spend much of my time in my house alone, except for personal care attendants and occasional visits from friends and family. My solitude, once a source of the blues for me, has now become, after much personal work, a source of strength. For it is when I am alone that I am most able to contact The Source from which I believe I come. It is that place, that experience, that sacred stillness, that brings me into immediate awareness that I am, in the most profound sense of the word, safe. Being alone by myself enables me to remember that I am never really alone; and my own company could not be more comforting."

While she would still just as soon be out in the world with people more often, Diane finds that her solitude is her daily path to spiritual inner peace. Without it, she doubts she could survive in this body. She has been able to live with multiple sclerosis for over twenty years by deeply internalizing the teaching of the Serenity Prayer.

"It simply doesn't work for me to expend energy on fighting things I cannot change," she said, "because nothing changes except that my energy is thereby depleted. As solitude began appearing to have become an unavoidable fixture in my life, I decided rather than feel negatively towards it, I could accept it and find a way to benefit from it."

Diane is a wonderful example of a woman who has accepted an extraordinarily difficult and unavoidable situation and has chosen to use it to deepen her spirituality.

Other women have also shared times in their lives when they have turned loneliness into precious solitude, a time for personal growth. A few women told me of times when their marriages broke up. They found themselves very lonely at first, but after a while, they were able to value that time alone and turn it into something very special.

There are women who find themselves in a relationship where their partner might spend long hours working or traveling, keeping them away from home. Other single women live alone and would prefer to be in a relationship.

"At any moment solitude may put on the face of loneliness," writes May Sarton. Our task is not to let ourselves sink into self-pity. The section on Active and Activities can be helpful. It's very important to connect with other people so that we maintain a balance in our lives.

When I ask for help, I know God gives me all the strength and courage I need in any situation. When I find myself in solitude that is not my choice, I can pray for acceptance, reach out to friends and community whenever possible, and use the time to grow spiritually and mentally. ▨

NATURE

I WANDERED LONELY AS A CLOUD
THAT FLOATS ON HIGH O'ER VALES AND HILLS,
WHEN ALL AT ONCE I SAW CROWD,
A HOST OF GOLDEN DAFFODILS:
BESIDE THE LAKE, BENEATH THE TREES,
FLUTTERING AND DANCING IN THE BREEZE. . . .
FOR OFT, WHEN ON MY COUCH I LIE
IN VACANT OR IN PENSIVE MOOD
THEY FLASH UPON THAT INWARD EYE
WHICH IS THE BLISS OF SOLITUDE;
AND THEN MY HEART WITH PLEASURE FILLS,
AND DANCES WITH THE DAFFODILS. ※

—WILLIAM WORDSWORTH

Watching the Tomatoes Grow

ALL MY LIFE THROUGH, THE NEW SIGHTS OF NATURE MADE
ME REJOICE LIKE A CHILD.

✧ MARIE CURIE

I was sitting outside on my deck one day when I heard a voice
in my mind say:

"What are you going to do, just sit and watch the tomatoes
grow?"

"No." I answered myself. "I'm not sitting all day and
watching the tomatoes grow. I'm just checking on the tomatoes.
I'm noticing that they're a little bigger today than they were
yesterday."

It was true. I had been staring, lost in the thought that the
tomatoes might be just a speck bigger. Nothing else was in my
consciousness. I was at total peace.

Sometimes I simply sit and stare at the waves coming in
and out at the beach, or at ripples in a pond, or leaves fluttering
like a dancer in the slightest breeze. I can become lost simply
watching a baby or a puppy play, a butterfly soar or a bumblebee
flit from blossom to blossom. And these also make fascinating
diversions for busy minds. These diversions are always so active,
appearing to have an important mission to accomplish.

I can become lost in my flower garden.

"I'm going out to check the flowers," I'd say to no one particular and out I go, studying each flower, checking for growth,

or their need for water, all the while marveling at how beautiful they are, each and every one of them.

First come solitude and silence. Then comes the delight in sharing with someone I care about. When friends drop by I love to show them my meditation garden, especially if I have added a new birdhouse or plant.

When my partner comes home from work I sometimes take her outside and show her the progress.

"See the tulips!" or

"Look how great the hydrangea is doing this year." or

"See how much the tomatoes have grown!"

Rachel Carson tells us that "Those who dwell, as scientists or laymen, among the beauties and mysteries of the earth are never alone or weary of life. . . . Those who contemplate the beauty of the earth find reserves of strength that will endure as long as life lasts."

Becoming mesmerized by nature's tiny details, being totally aware with all our senses for just a few minutes can restore balance to a scattered mind and rest to an exhausted body.

Today I will take at least five minutes, more if I can, to rest my mind and my body experiencing nature. I will take time to get better acquainted with nature. ❈

Nature's Comfort

FOR EVERYTHING THERE IS A SEASON,
AND A TIME TO EVERY PURPOSE UNDER THE HEAVEN.

❧ ECCLESIATES

Studying nature can teach us so much about our own lives. Just as there is constant change in the universe, so are there predictable consistencies in nature's changes. We can depend on the changes of seasons, of spring following winter, of fall following summer. We can count on the tides going in and out twice in every twenty-four hours. The moon makes predictable cycles, as does the earth spinning around the sun.

While these routine changes are taking place, beyond our control and without any help from us, nature is busy acting out in a seemingly inconsistent manner, affecting our lives with rainbows and hurricanes, earthquakes and sunshine, heavy rains and drought.

We have our own highs and lows, ups and downs, joys and sorrows. What happens between the predictable is unpredictable and uncontrollable. Taking time to be alone with nature, connecting with a power greater than ourselves on a regular basis, can be an anchor in times of difficulty, a comfort in times of pain, and a friend in times of joy and happiness. There is reassurance in knowing that the mountains and oceans are always available as a refuge to pacify and sustain us. The sun and the breeze can feel as if someone is holding us. William Wordsworth tells us to "come forth into the light of things, let Nature be your teacher."

Being close to nature helps us to feel connected and a part of something greater than ourselves. Many people feel closer to God in nature. There is a wonderful proverb that tells us, "Every blade of grass has its share of the dews of heaven." Saint Francis of Assisi wrote that a single sunbeam is enough to drive away many shadows.

Life happens. And when it feels as if the rug has been pulled out from under us, when we feel we're being pushed to places we don't want to go by eighty-mile-an-hour winds, we can remember. These are the places in between the rainbows and that our times in precious solitude strengthen our spirits through all the changing seasons of our lives. They remind us that rainbows and sunbeams will return.

Today I affirm that nothing is forever and I can find strength no matter what is going on in my life in nature and in God. ❧

Getting Lost in Nature Even When You Can't Get Outside!

ALL NATURE WEARS ONE UNIVERSAL GRIN.

❧ TOM THUMB THE GREAT

Getting lost in nature can be so enriching. It can heal our minds, bodies, and spirits. Being one with whatever it is we are experiencing with all our senses refreshes, heals, and brings peace. Author Lorraine Anderson writes, "Nature has been for me, for as long as I can remember, a source of solace, inspiration, adventure, and delight; a home, a teacher, a companion."

But what happens if we can't get outside? What if we have to work for a living, take care of a sick friend or relative, or stay in with the child who has chickenpox? What happens when we are sick or the weather is stormy? We can bring nature to us in a number of ways, maybe not quite as satisfying as being out of doors, but certainly fulfilling and relaxing.

Poets have written millions of words for us to help us feel the immeasurable joys of nature. "God, I can push the grass apart and lay my finger on Thy heart!" wrote Edna St. Vincent Millay. "Forget not that the earth delights to feel your bare feet and the winds long to play with your hair," said Khalil Gibran. These two lines can open our hearts and help us to feel we are out there, pushing the grass apart or feeling the wind in our hair. If we can't get out of doors, we can spend some time in solitude bringing nature into our lives through poetry and prose. These moments of reading can offer a surprising richness to a day that might otherwise be a dull, stuck-indoors day.

Water fountains are so soothing and restful. We can become lost for minutes or hours watching and listening to the flow of the water from a fountain in our home. It's not necessary to spend a lot of money on a fancy fountain. Prices range anywhere from very expensive down to only nineteen dollars. An outdoor fountain can be thoughtfully placed so it can be watched from a window on days you are inside. Outside gardens, too, can offer peace and joy from a window view.

There are many ways we can connect with nature and experience its greatness, even indoors. Take a few moments to water your plants, repot an overgrown plant, or watch the leaves or rain or snow outside your window. Plant seeds and grow an indoor garden. Force bulbs and feel the joy of their bloom long before they break through the earth outdoors. Build a terrarium. Add a greenhouse to your kitchen window. Grow herbs on your kitchen windowsill. I feel uplifted and excited every time I cut dill from my own plant to use in a recipe.

Whether we have five minutes or five hours, whether we are inside or out outside, we can find time for solitude in nature.

I can add to the ways I can connect with nature indoors, preparing myself for the days when I can't go out. ▨

The Healing Powers of Nature

WHEN SOMETHING INTOLERABLE IS IN MY LIFE, I HEAD FOR THE WATER. IT LEAVENS ME IN SOME WAY. SOME MIDDLE-MOST PART OF ME IS SOOTHED AND SILENCED BY IT.

ॐ ALICE KOLLER

I learned the word "biophilia," an exciting new psychological theory, for the first time when reading Sarah Ban Breathnach's wonderful book *Simple Abundance*. It creates a word for something we all feel—a deep attraction to nature. Pulitzer Prize–winning biologist Edward O. Wilson believes our biophilia urges—"the love of living things"—plants, wildlife, and the great outdoors is genetic, encoded in human beings to ensure balance, harmony, and preservation. Dr. Wilson reports "Attraction to natural environments is not simply a cultural phenomenon. There is evidence it is a deeper, biological urge." Millions of years ago we survived as hunters and food gatherers. Spotting one small animal could make the difference between eating and going hungry, explains Dr. Wilson.

Sarah also writes that there are therapists who specialize in "ecopsychology" believing that "deepening our emotional ties to nature is as vital to our well being as the close personal bonds we pursue with family and friends."

One of the ways my friend Margie Levine recovered from devastating disease was by connecting with nature in her own backyard. She spent time every day listening to the birds, kneeling on the earth, and feeling its connection with her body. In her apartment in the city, where she was not as close to the earth, she sat in solitude outside on her balcony, looking at trees and imagining that she was sitting up in their branches.

Everyday still she goes outside in nature for at least three minutes. She believes that this helps her to reach a deeper state of consciousness, an alpha state, where it is easier to connect with the Divine Source. Getting into a regular pattern, she goes out as often as possible for little pieces of time each day.

People are drawn to nature for healing. We can find solace hibernating in a cave, walking along the beach, climbing to the top of the mountain to pray and meditate, gliding in a canoe on a clear pond, hiking in the woods, weeding our garden, or taking a walk in the park.

In his book *The Celestine Prophecy*, James Redfield discussed how certain environments radiate more energy than others, such as old natural environments, especially forests. His third insight elaborated on the beauty of nature. "When you appreciate the beauty and uniqueness of things, you receive energy."

One of the things I heard after my son died was that there was healing in hugging a tree. I had no idea whether or not there was any truth in this, but I was willing to try anything. The idea is that everything is full of energy and that trees are something substantial that we can feel with our entire bodies. They are alive and growing and very powerful. There are many trees behind my house. When I was sure no one was looking, I found a large tree and put my arms around it. Holding myself close to the trunk, it actually felt good.

We can take mini-breaks during the day or night to connect with nature by spending a few moments looking out the window, watching the clouds, sky, moon, or stars. If an outside view of nature isn't available to us, we can create our own indoor garden with potted plants and spend some time with them.

I feel powerful healing energy when I connect with nature. I am making sure I take the time to make this a regular part of my day. ▓

Gardening

THE KISS OF SUN FOR PARDON,
THE SONG OF THE BIRDS FOR MIRTH,
ONE IS NEARER GOD'S HEART IN A GARDEN
THAN ANYWHERE ELSE ON EARTH.

❧ DOROTHY GURNEY, "GOD'S GARDEN," POEMS (1913)

There was a time when we thought about selling our house. Giving up the garden was one of the hardest things for me to consider. How could I leave without seeing what came up the next spring? Would the tulips, the crocuses, and the daffodils bloom? Would there be more flowers from the same bulbs? Would the perennials be larger? Would the annuals, such as pansies, which are supposed to live for only one season, return again, as they sometimes do?

Thoughts such as these kept popping up until, gratefully, I accepted that I was gardening for the pleasure of gardening. Feeling and smelling the earth, studying the best place to plant the next bulb, simply being out of doors, aware of the miracle of growth, continuity of life, and how we are all part of the same miracle.

I love the way my body feels after hours of gardening, exhausted, worn, hardly able to move, filled with aches and pains. Yet I feel so good! How could I feel so exhilarated when I ache so? I think it is because the joy of the accomplishment fills my spirit. I use every part of my body. It is stretched in ways I thought impossible to accomplish the digging, the pruning, and whatever else needs to be done. I could still do it! I wasn't too old! I knew, if I gardened year after year, I would keep my body in shape, doing what I loved so much.

I finally came to the "aha!" realization that if and when we did move, I could have a patio or a deck and plant flowers in containers, maybe even expanding into vegetables. I immediately experimented by growing tomato plants and herbs in pots on my deck. I filled two planters boxes with brightly colored flowers such as petunias and dahlias. My step-daughter gave me an artichoke plant to add to my collection. A cherry tomato plant grew so large I had to tie it to the uprights of the deck to hold it up.

I've learned so many lessons! I came to see that I didn't have to depend on the old way, just because I always did it that way. I could, if necessary, downsize and enjoy nature just as much on a smaller scale.

There is such happiness in gardening throughout seasons. At the end of winter, while snow is still on the ground, early crocuses can be seen pushing their way up through the cold hard soil to smile at the sun. They bring such pleasure. Daffodils come next, then hyacinths, tulips, and on and on, through the spring, summer, and fall, keeping me busy, keeping me happy.

Many women have told me that gardening is their favorite activity in solitude. Phyllis Theroux has written that what hooks one on gardening is that it is the closest one can come to being present at the Creation.

Whether I water a small plant on my windowsill, or spend hours weeding out of doors, I will cherish my time with my garden today! ▨

Nature's Tranquilizers

ONE OF MY MOST MEMORABLE MOMENTS OF SOLITUDE IS STANDING UNDERNEATH A 200-YEAR-OLD BEECH TREE IN THE EVENING, JUST AS THE LAST SNOWFLAKES GENTLY FALL ON MY HAIR, CHEEKS AND EYELASHES IN A SILENCE THAT ONLY A CALM NEWLY SNOW-COVERED EARTH CAN PROVIDE.

ANN WOLFE

After writing at my computer for some time one beautiful May morning, I knew it was time to stop and turn to other work. I had a huge to-do list and time was running out. The thought of doing those things began to overwhelm me. I felt as if I were ready to explode. I wanted to scream! I had visions of throwing all my papers across the room.

The out of doors was calling me. My garden and the unplanted new plants were calling me. The soft spring breeze said "Come on out! Feel me on your face. Let me blow your cares away. Put your hands in the earth and get close to God."

One side of me battled the old, "No. I have too much to do. I'll go out in a few hours," while another voice argued, "You've been waiting all winter for a day like today. How many Saturdays and Sundays and evenings have you worked? You can't go out for a few hours?" "Just one more call!" I rebutted. "I'll go out then." "Now," I demanded of myself. "It could be cloudy by then."

My conflict grew stronger and I felt more and more overwhelmed. I could feel the pressure within me grow. I eventually gave in to the fact that I was accomplishing nothing by staying in that could not be handled when I had helped myself to some of nature's joy.

As soon as the decision was made, I felt a tremendous sense of relief. I was going outside! Out of doors, no matter where, is one of my very favorite places, as long as the temperature is above 45 or 50 degrees and it's not raining or snowing.

I was going to use solitude as an escape, as a mind-stopping, pressure-releasing a natural tranquilizer. And what a wonderful choice it was! The sun and the breeze were my companions as I dug and watered and planted in my garden. I stopped often to listen to the large variety of birds that visit our property, taking great delight when I could identify one of them. I filled the bird bath with water and made sure the feeder had a good supply of birdseed. I shooed away a squirrel every time he came close to the feeder. I watched the ongoing battle of a pair of song sparrows fighting for the custody of their birdhouse as a wren tried to take it away from them.

I rushed into the house at 4:30, just in time to write out two checks and get them into the post office before it closed. That fulfilled my sense of responsibility and added to my peace of mind.

Mine was definitely an escape to solitude! No lofty goals of spirituality or being at one with the universe. No looking within to connect with my inner strength. I was simply being alone in a place I loved, finding joy doing the things I loved to do. Escaping from my self-created, screaming task master to the wonderful world of peace and quiet out of doors. What really could be more spiritual than finding inner peace through the natural world around me?

Today I am going to take time alone with nature today and do something I love just for me. ✖

ACTIVE
SOLITUDE

When I dance, I dance; when I sleep, I sleep; yes, and when I walk alone in a beautiful orchard, if my thoughts drift to far-off matters for some part of the time, for some other part I lead them back again to the walk, the orchard, to the sweetness of this solitude, to myself. ✖

ANONYMOUS

Mini-Mindfulness Breaks

MINDFULNESS IS THE MIRACLE BY WHICH WE MASTER AND RESTORE OURSELVES.

❧ THICH NHAT HNAH

There are times when days get so full that anything more than taking ten minutes alone feels impossible. Some days it might seem too hard to squeeze in even ten minutes. At times like these, mini breaks can be refreshing. Ten minutes here and five minutes there can change the mood of our day and turn what might have been a pressure keg experience into a more bearable one.

Mindfulness, simply being fully present with whatever is going on in the moment, can be a wonderful break and can make ten minutes feel much longer. We can experiment with something we do everyday. For example, we can bring our full attention to brushing our teeth. When I am not being mindful of what I am doing, I am thinking of hundreds of other things. I'm either in the past, rehashing a conversation I just had, or in the future planning my day. When I am not mindful I finish brushing my teeth without even knowing I brushed them. But when I am mindful, I can stop, instead, and be in the moment. I can listen to the sound of the water, smell the toothpaste, feel the tooth brush against my gums, and feel the taste of the toothpaste.

We can experiment while in the shower, listening to the water and being aware of how it feels as it flows over our bodies. We can smell the soap and feel it in our hands and on our bodies. We can even make a cup with the palms of our hands and catch the water. In both activities we can watch our mind going away from what we are doing and bring it back again. As in meditation, each time we notice we are away from what we are doing, we simply bring our attention back to the present moment.

While washing the dishes probably doesn't feel like quality time in solitude, it can be! Author Thich Nhat Hanh suggests that we practice mindfulness with everything that we do, including washing the dishes. He writes "There are two ways to wash the dishes. The first is to wash the dishes in order to have clean dishes and the second is to wash the dishes in order to wash the dishes." The first is hurrying through it to get it done. Thich Nhat Hahn tells us that if we are doing them just to get them done, they are a nuisance. "What's more, we are not alive during the time we are washing the dishes. In fact we are incapable of realizing the miracle of life while standing at the sink . . . we are incapable of actually living one minute of life.

When we are not lost in thoughts or daydreams the moments feel longer and more peaceful. Bringing our awareness to whatever we are doing in the present moment, at least a few times a day, especially in busy times when we can't take a longer break, can be very peaceful. It could be during the time when we are walking to the car or stopping for a cup of coffee. Eventually, we can get into the habit of being mindful of everything we do! That's when, as Thich Nhat Hanh tells us, we have peace within us at all times.

I am learning to be fully present and connected to what I am doing in each moment. I feel more alive and energized when I take mini-mindfulness breaks. ▓

Unexpected Walking Lessons

GRACE IS FOUND IN OUR CAPACITY TO LISTEN INWARDLY AND TO TRUST THAT LISTENING.

❧ CHRISTINA FELDMAN

It was a beautiful August morning. The sky was a brilliant blue with just a touch of small wispy clouds occasionally gliding by. I was out for my morning walk, thoroughly enjoying myself, aware of how good it felt to move my body, delighting in the day. There was a soft breeze blowing against my hair and cooling my skin.

I was aware of my arms swinging in rhythm with my footsteps. I noticed that if I thought about my arms, they would feel awkward and get out of rhythm but by just letting them swing naturally, they swayed back and forth in a relaxed, easy rhythm.

Three or four minutes into the walk, I felt a sharp pain on the right side of my left foot from poison ivy that had been giving me a lot of trouble. The pain increased. Should I give up the walk? Would my sneaker and sock rub against the blisters and break them, spreading the poison ivy to other parts of my foot? I remember a doctor telling me that poison ivy couldn't spread that way, but could I trust him? All my thoughts went into what was happening inside my left shoe. I had lost complete awareness of the beauty of the day and the wonderful feeling I had experienced just a few minutes earlier.

The pain stayed as I struggled to decide what to do. I chose to continue the walk, live with the pain, and enjoy my outing as well as I could. After a while the flash of a bird caught my eye. A car went by and the driver smiled. I saw a man working in his garden. The caress of the breeze became apparent again.

The pain had lessened. I imagined that this meant that the blister had broken. Again I was concerned that the poison ivy would spread. Now thoughts went to the life lesson I was learning. Always choices. How do we know what is the right choice? I had heard that "the moment of ultimate certainty never arrives."

There was a time in my life when I would not consider staying with any pain, whether it was emotional or physical. I would run away from it, hide from it, or deny it. My old way, twenty-five years ago, was usually with alcohol. We all have our own ways whether it is with food, work, other addictions, or denial.

Just from this morning walk I learned that:

I always have choices.

It was worth the pain to be able to experience the joy.

Nothing stays the same. Everything changes. Joy had changed to pain and then had changed back to joy again, when I stopped struggling against the pain.

When I focused on my pain, I lost the beauty of the moment.

A smile from a stranger can warm my heart.

When I worried about the broken blisters, I wasn't having fun!

The fear that the blisters would break was only in my mind. When I got home and took my sneaker and sock off, the blisters were intact. They had not leaked at all!

Life isn't always perfect.

The pain disappointed my expectations of a good walk.

All these lessons were certainly not new. Most of this I already understood. Nor were they earth-shattering lessons. I keep learning to live life in an easier, gentler way. What was truly reinforced in this walk is that if I had not taken the time for my precious solitude, I would not have had these experiences and the lessons it gave me. If I had chosen to stop my walk because of the pain I would have missed the healthy exercise, the peaceful time with nature, and the feeling of accomplishment that a walk can bring.

I am strengthening my inner spirit, building my self-esteem, and deepening my spiritual foundation by choosing to take time to nurture myself. ▓

Stop! Sit for Just a Minute

ONLY IN THE REALITY OF THE PRESENT CAN WE LOVE, CAN WE AWAKEN, CAN WE FIND PEACE AND UNDERSTANDING AND CONNECTION WITH OURSELVES AND THE WORLD.

※ JACK KORNFIELD

The other day I went over to the house of my friend Libby, who was helping me with some work. I was late and rushing to get in and get out. She, too, was rushing as she was going out of town on the following day and needed to pack.

"Stop. Sit for a minute," she said.

"I can't. I really have to go. I haven't got the time," I answered.

"Stop." she said, "Sit for a minute."

I looked at her and said "I can't" and remained standing.

She said. "Stop. Sit for just a moment."

So I sat down and took a moment to look around and see the flowers she had taken time to plant around her porch. They were beautiful. And I took the time to see how very, very beautiful my friend's eyes are. They're a very deep, deep blue and really quite exquisite.

I took the time to visit a few moments. Before I knew it ten minutes had gone by and I was feeling much more relaxed, much more peaceful, and so was she.

I am so grateful that I took the time to stop.

My friend gave me a gift of time. Had it not been for her I would have rushed in and rushed out, gotten in my car and sped away, on to the next thing on my list. She gave me the gift of being present for ten minutes, ten minutes which I would have missed had I kept going.

Author and meditation teacher Thich Nhat Hahn reminds us that if we think peace and happiness are elsewhere and we run after them, we'll never arrive. He says that only when we realize that peace and happiness are available in the present moment will we be able to relax. He advises us to just stop! "Touch the ground of the present moment deeply, and you will touch real peace and joy."

We do not always need to be alone in solitude to come to a place of peace and renewal. We can find quiet time with our friends or our pets. My friend Joy can relax and let go when she is alone with her dogs. It's the only time she can slow down. They don't ask anything of her. They don't expect anything. She finds pure love and peace when she is with them.

Lauren, a nurse practioner, takes one day off a week, no matter what, from her busy schedule. She finds great comfort being alone with her horse. She feels she is in a loving space, as she gently grooms and talks to her.

When was the last time you took the time to stop?

Today I will take some time to stop, no matter how busy I am. I will take time to appreciate the moment. ▧

Birdwatching and Other Solitary Activities in a Crowd

IT IS EASY IN THE WORLD TO LIVE WITH THE WORLD'S OPINION; IT IS EASY IN SOLITUDE TO LIVE AFTER YOUR OWN; BUT THE GREAT MAN IS HE WHO IN THE MIDST OF THE CROWD KEEPS WITH PERFECT SWEETNESS THE INDEPENDENCE OF SOLITUDE.

❧ RALPH WALDO EMERSON

Birdwatching is an activity that can be done with other people and still be a source of solitude, says author and therapist Sandy Bierig. She finds birdwatching a solitary adventure, taking her totally away from everything else. One can become so absorbed in identifying each species, keeping track of the number of birds one finds in each species, naming them, and recording them that it doesn't matter how many other people are in the same area.

Sandy finds birdwatching nourishing and balancing. As a therapist who spends a great deal of time with other people, birdwatching fills her need to get away and find quiet time connecting with nature. She calls it a "respectable form of loitering."

Years ago Sandy discovered Great Meadows, a very special birdwatching place for her in Concord, Massachusetts. There are rarely other people there, and when there are, they never bother each other. The place is so quiet and peaceful that Sandy brings up images of it whenever she wants to find peace within herself. She finds solitude by nurturing her soul, mind, and heart. She suggests if you can't get outside, window bird feeders or feeders set on posts in the yard can also bring great pleasure.

Kate Mitchell is a busy lawyer and home builder who often takes guided hikes in the mountains. She finds solitude in motion most fulfilling. Hiking in the woods or backpacking in the mountains takes her outside to the beauty of the natural world. While a junior in college, she climbed her first mountain, Mt. Monadnock, with friends. It was an incredibly gorgeous day and she felt totally connected with God, the source and sacredness of her life.

Kate feels her interconnectedness with all of life when hiking. It is a time to check in with herself, get in touch with her own personal needs, and return to her center. What she finds in solitude is a willingness to just be and let go of all definitions of herself as a human being. Within the context of aching joints, bugs, blisters, cold drinks when you want them hot, Kate finds extraordinary joy, contentment, and peace.

She finds this is all still true even when she hikes with a group. She can remain in her own space and feel in synch with herself.

"Our deepest wishes are whispers of our deeper selves. We must learn to respect them. We must learn to listen," advises author Sarah Ban Breathnach. There are so many ways we can follow our hearts into activities that bring us joy. We can find fulfillment in so many different directions, experiment in limitless ways using our bodies, our minds, or our creativity.

Swimming, canoeing, kyacking, skiing, basket weaving, painting, photography, and fishing are just a few of the many activities we can do while others are present but that allow us to feel we are in a space apart.

Finding activities that we can do with others while maintaining our own sense of solitude is a wonderful gift for everyone. We can feel close and at the same time separate, some part of us knowing we are sharing a very special experience together, and yet at another level not even aware that anyone else exists.

I am following where my heart takes me, finding joy in so many places I never thought possible. ▓

Walking

HE WALKS WITH NATURE; AND HER PATHS ARE PEACE.

✣ AUTHOR UNKNOWN

Many people have told me that their favorite way of enjoying solitude is by walking. My friend Sarah loves to walk in the woods on Cape Cod with her dog Mutley. The day after she told me that walking was her favorite form of solitude she e-mailed me the following: "I just found out yesterday that my dog has bone cancer. As we speak, they are doing a biopsy. The vet has suggested that he have his leg amputated and although this won't save his life, it will make his last months fairly painless for him. He is his normal jubilant self, except not as often as he was before. Except for his inability to put weight on his leg, he just doesn't seem sick. Anyway, we're both so sad; it's hard to imagine our lives without this dog. He has gotten me through such awful times and makes me so happy. It occurred to me that dogs bring out the best in us, because we get to practice unconditional love almost perfectly."

After making many inquiries and discovering that most dogs can do very well on three legs, Sarah decided to proceed with the operation.

A few weeks later she e-mailed again, "We've been going into the woods almost everyday and Mutlet barrels up and down the hills on his three legs! He does get tired out—or maybe just hot— so we don't walk as long as we used to, but it has been really fun watching his progress. We get lots of inquiries about his health, friends offering to dog-sit and bring dog snacks like peanut butter flavor rawhide. One friend who has terminal cancer herself has come over twice to do Reike on him and bless him with water!" Through all this she kept on walking.

One day, while in Newport, Rhode Island, I decided to take my morning walk past the beautiful mansions on Bellevue Avenue. I walked at my regular pace and noticed a woman in front of me walking very slowly. As I passed her I saw that she was perhaps twenty years older than I. I could still be walking when I reached her age. "That will be my speed in twenty years," I thought. A few minutes later a woman perhaps twenty years younger than me came jogging by, passing me easily. "She is what I used to be," I thought. I got lost in the idea of the three generations of women as a continuum of life, what I was, what I am, and what I might be in the future. All three of us were connected, yet separate.

There are lessons to be learned and gifts to be found everywhere if only we are open to them when they occur. There is a wonderful line in *The Color Purple* by Alice Walker, "I think it pisses God off if you walk by the color purple in a field somewhere and don't notice it." Even on a crowded street in a busy city, a few minutes of conscious walking can change your mood, release stress, and bring balance and serenity.

Today I am practicing being aware of my surroundings and the gifts I can find in them. ✻

Create a Meditation Garden

HERE IS THE GREAT MYSTERY OF LIFE AND GROWTH.
EVERYTHING IS CHANGING, GROWING, AIMING AT SOME-
THING, BUT SILENTLY, UNBOASTFULLY, TAKING ITS TIME.

❧ RUTH STOUT

One of the most delightful things I ever did for myself was to create a meditation garden. It has given me so much pleasure. Off to the side of my house I cleared a section of underbrush and weeds. Then I dug out a small, shallow hole, maybe two by four feet wide and eight inches deep. I lined the hole with some blue plastic I had in my garage, placed rocks along the edge to hold it down and then filled it with water. Then, I set flagstone all around the little pool so I could take a meditative walk around it.

The planning, digging, and weeding took a long time, over a period of several years. Poison ivy had flourished long before I started and, careful as I tried to be, I still spent many weeks trying one remedy or another to get rid of the incredible itch. But it didn't stop me. I went back each year to clear out more of the poison ivy so I could have a safe walk.

Gradually I added two birdhouses that I had painted in the winter, two chairs and many plants and bulbs. My daughters gave me delightful stepping stones with sayings chiseled into them that read, "Welcome the hope that flowers bring," and "An hour in the garden puts life's problems in perspective."

There is great joy in designing and creating such a garden, and the peace and serenity are ongoing. I can sit and read, weed the garden, walk around the small pool, write, or simply sit and meditate or think. It is a sacred place to me. A meditation garden combines both active and inactive solitude, giving us a choice of whatever we want in the moment.

My friend Judy went a few steps further, building a waterfall with rocks, slate, and a pump. She added a filter to the pond, which is large and deep enough to house goldfish. The sound of the water and the addition of the ritual of daily feeding add delightfully to her times in solitude.

Perhaps you don't have the space for a meditation garden or even the inclination to go to all that work. Then a zen garden is wonderful to make for indoor use! Collect small stones and pebbles of various sizes, shapes and colors. Find a flat box such as an old gift box and fill it part way with sand. You can use different colors and textures of sand and use a small rake made out of a twig to form it into interesting designs. Then add your stones and pebbles in any way you find interesting.

Zen gardens are very delicate and beautiful, full of simplicity and harmony. They are built on the principle of wabi-sabi, a Japanese expression for beauty found in certain objects, such as weathered wood and rocks.

Place your zen garden somewhere you will see it everyday such as on your desk or a table. You can change the design and rake the sand in your time in solitude. You can have a lot of pleasure creating it and recreating it, spending countless hours sitting quietly by it and meditating.

I can slow down and appreciate how just a few moments in my garden can help me become centered and composed. ▓

INACTIVE,
QUIET SOLITUDE

IF YOU CAN SPEND A PERFECTLY USELESS AFTERNOON IN A PERFECTLY USELESS MANNER, YOU HAVE LEARNED HOW TO LIVE. ▚

LIN YU-T'ANG

Meditation

*THE SECRET OF MEDITATION IS TO BECOME CONSCIOUS
OF EACH MOMENT OF YOUR EXISTENCE.*

꙳ THICH NHAT HAHN

The practice of meditation has completely changed my life. I have found a peace and relaxation I didn't know possible. My first experience was with Transcendental Meditation, popularly known as TM. By quietly saying a phrase, or mantra, over and over again to ourselves, we are able to quiet the thoughts that go on in our minds and to come to a place of peace.

Later I discovered Insight Meditation, known also as mindfulness, which I have been practicing ever since. Mindfulness is a practice of quieting down our thoughts and being fully present in each moment. I discuss it in more detail in the next section.

Meditation can be a time to empty our mind or still our thoughts, a time to become centered and balanced. It is time when we connect with a deeper place in ourselves, our soul, our inner spirit, the God within, or the higher energies of the universe.

It has been said that in prayer we talk to God and in meditation we listen. Ambrose wrote: "Prayer is the wing wherewith the soul flies to heaven, and meditation the eye wherewith we see God."

Meditation is a spiritual practice. One can meditate and not be religious and yet meditation is a part of most religions. Most important, it's a deeply personal experience.

One of my favorite teachers, author and retreat leader Christina Feldman, tells us that "to undertake a period of meditation is to offer a gift to yourself. It is an act of caring for your own well-being and consciously nurturing inner connection. It is a time of exploring the most intimate relationship of your life—your relationship with yourself. It is helpful to approach these times with deep sensitivity and care so that they may be times of enrichment." She writes that grace is found in our capacity to listen inwardly and to trust in that listening.

Meditation has become more and more popular in the West since the 1970s, and there are hundreds of books that can teach you the many ways that you can meditate. Workshops and retreats are offered just about everywhere. You can't go into a local health food store without seeing posters and advertisements of upcoming events that teach or include meditation.

Material possessions such as houses, cars, and jewelry make us feel good for the moment, but in the long run, we have a deeper longing inside, a spiritual longing that no person or thing can satisfy. Some of us turn to alcohol or drugs, excitement, sex, or dozens of other experiences to fill this emptiness. They, too, bring some satisfaction, but it is only temporary. Soon we want more and more of what makes us feel good and we want to push away our pain and discomfort. Mediation can bring us to that deeper spiritual connection that fills that emptiness.

If you are new to meditation, lessons are a good way to begin. Find a teacher or a group. Ask around. You will be amazed at how many people will have suggestions for you. It's always helpful to practice regularly with an ongoing weekly group.

Experiment with different forms of meditation. See what feels right to you. Take time in solitude to give yourself the gift of meditation, to develop a daily practice for which you take time, no matter what else is going on in your life.

Meditation is a gift I give myself regularly, knowing how important it is for me spiritually. In meditation I connect with a quiet place deep within me where I find peace and connect with my Higher Power. ▦

Mindfulness

MINDFULNESS IS THE AWARE, BALANCED ACCEPTANCE OF THE PRESENT EXPERIENCE. IT ISN'T MORE COMPLICATED THAN THAT. IT IS THE OPENING TO OR RECEIVING THE PRESENT MOMENT, PLEASANT OR UNPLEASANT, JUST AS IT IS, WITHOUT EITHER CLINGING TO IT OR REJECTING IT.

❧ SYLVIA BOORSTEIN

Wouldn't it be wonderful if we could simply be in the moment, without the feeling that something is either right or wrong, without judgments or prejudices? Wouldn't it be wonderful if we could simply accept whatever is going on in the moment and feel the peace that comes from such acceptance? Instead of beating ourselves up or praising ourselves by telling ourselves that something is good or bad, right or wrong, pleasant or unpleasant, we simply could say, "Oh. This is what it is," and continue to go on with what we are doing.

Mindfulness is one of the many forms of meditation. It brings us clarity and wisdom. I don't mean that we accept without further action whatever is going on in our lives. If someone is being abused, we do whatever we can to stop it. If a child is running out into the street we run after her and pull her back. By being present with whatever is going on in the present moment, we see what action, if any, needs to be taken.

We use the terms *the practice of mindfulness* or *the practice of meditation* because it is simply just that, a practice. Just as we practice the piano, dancing, or anything that requires repetition to gain skills, we practice mindfulness by sitting with our breath, noticing what takes us away from our breath, and returning to our breath, for one or more periods each day.

My favorite definition of mindfulness, or insight meditation as it is also called, is from a brochure from the Insight Meditation Society in Barre, Massachusetts:

> Insight meditation is a simple and direct prac-
> tice—the moment to moment investigation of the
> mind–body process through calm and focused
> awareness. Learning to experience from a place of
> stillness enables one to relate to life with less fear
> and less clinging. Seeing life as a constantly
> changing process, one begins to accept pleasure
> and pain, fear and joy and all aspects of life with
> increasing equanimity and balance. As insight
> deepens, wisdom and compassion arise. Insight
> meditation is a way of seeing clearly the totality of
> one's being and experience. Growth in clarity
> brings about penetrating insight into the nature of
> who we are and increased peace in our daily lives.

The key word to my understanding mindfulness medita-
tion here is *awareness*. Awareness is consciousness, insight, knowledge, and wakefulness.

Its purpose is to be fully awake and aware in each moment, to discover the essence of who we are, to get in touch with all the blocks that keep us from touching our inner spirit and listening to the guidance of our soul.

Author Pema Chodron writes that "Everything in our lives can help us to wake up or to fall asleep, and basically it's up to us to let it wake us up." She says that with awareness, you are able to find out for yourself what causes misery and what causes happiness.

Today I will be fully awake! I will bring my awareness into everything I do. ✻

Bringing Meditation into Our Entire Lives

IF WE ARE REALLY ENGAGED IN MINDFULNESS. . . A JOY WILL
OPEN OUR HEART LIKE A FLOWER, ENABLING US TO ENTER
INTO THE WORD OF REALITY.

❧ THICH NHAT HANH

Meditation begins with a daily sitting practice. We stop all out-side activity and sit quietly. As we develop the practice to stop and look inside, and it becomes more and more a part of our lives, we also find ourselves stopping and looking outside. Deepak Chopra tells us, "Be willing to follow the clues of the spirit, meditate to find the pure silence within yourself, know that the goal of spirit is true and worth pursuing."

We can find peace in stopping to examine the smallest leaf, look into the most intricate flower, watch a bumblebee flit from blossom to blossom, keep our focus on one single snowflake as it slowly falls to the ground. We become better listeners, less self-absorbed, more open to share.

In her book *When Things Fall Apart,* Pema Chodron shares the simple directions a grandmother told her grandchildren when she took them on a walk to see animals. She said "If you sit still, you'll see something. If you're very quiet, you'll hear something." This is what our practice brings us. We can find peace in each moment. Pema goes on to say that, "This fundamental richness is available in each moment. The key is to relax, relax to a cloud in the sky. . . relax to the sound of the telephone ringing."

Another example is practicing a slow meditative walk as you are walking to and from your car. This can be a wonderful transition from work to home or vice versa, leaving work at work or concerns you have at home by being in the present moment. Rather than being off somewhere in your head, lost in your thoughts, thinking and planning, bring your full awareness to the present moment. Feel your feet in your shoes, touching the ground, as your arms are swinging and your body is moving.

Even on a crowded street or at a busy beach, walking meditation can help to slow you down, to become centered again, and to keep you in the present moment. This can bring you a deep sense of peace.

Today I am finding more and more opportunities to bring the peace and quiet I find in meditation to other parts of my day. ▦

Bringing Mindfulness to Our Thoughts

TO BE CONSCIOUS THAT WE ARE PERCEIVING OR THINKING IS TO BE CONSCIOUS OF OUR OWN EXISTENCE.

❧ ARISTOTLE

Imagine something coming up in the future that makes you nervous. Perhaps you are having an exam, a public speaking presentation, or an operation. Feel how your body responds to this thought. Are you holding your breath? Does your stomach tighten or turn over? Where do you hold your fears?

Now bring your attention to a time when you felt great joy. Again, feel how your body responds to this memory. Is there a different expression on your face? Is your body more relaxed? Is your breath different? By bringing our attention to these feelings, they tend to lose their power over us. When we open up to the awareness of the present moment and breathe into it, the feelings wash away and we can feel peace. Take time in solitude to study the way you respond to your thoughts and feelings. Be gentle and loving with yourself. This is a wonderful way to get to know yourself.

How many times have you been driving and suddenly realized that you didn't remember driving from one place to another? How often do you find yourself in a conversation suddenly realizing that you haven't heard part of what the speaker was saying to you? Your mind has been either off in a day-dream or wondering what you are going to say next, or judging what is being said to you. Maybe it went away remembering something in the past or worried about something coming up in the future?

A daily practice of meditation helps to develop concentration and focus. It helps to train your mind to be in the moment, to bring your full attention to what is going on in the moment. You can become more focused, have better concentration. You can become a better listener and a friend by totally being present with another person.

The word *Budh* in the Indian Sanskrit language means "to wake up, to know." Buddha means "the Awakened or Enlightened One," and all Buddhist teachings try to share the Buddha's experience of awakening to truth. The Buddha discovered that the world was full of suffering and that there was a way to end suffering. Mindfulness is the path to end suffering.

When we bring mindfulness into our entire lives we also become aware of the thoughts that create our suffering. We can see more clearly when we are holding on to anger, resentments, guilt, and all other emotions that lead us to pain. We learn by experiencing the feelings that are connected with our thoughts, by observing the mind–body connection.

It is so powerful to know that I can bring more peace and love into my life by practicing meditation. I am learning to become gentle and loving with myself. I am learning to let go of my suffering. ❈

Walking Meditation

WALKING MINDFULLY ON THE EARTH CAN RESTORE OUR PEACE AND HARMONY, AND IT CAN RESTORE THE EARTH'S PEACE AND HARMONY AS WELL.

❧ THICH NHAT HAHN

I learned a formal walking meditation many years ago from my teacher Larry Rosenberg in Cambridge, Massachusetts. Forty or fifty serious meditation students met with him once a week for an eight-week beginner's class to learn Insight Meditation. The class was held in a large room with cushions arranged in a wide circle. When we entered the room, everyone stopped talking. The silence brought an immediate sense of peace to me after a hectic day at work.

Each class began with twenty minutes of sitting meditation, followed by a twenty minute walking meditation, consisting of four basic steps: lifting one's foot, moving it, placing that foot on the ground, and then shifting one's weight on to it. These four steps are then repeated with the other foot, all as slowly as possible. All concentration is placed on lifting, moving, placing, and shifting. Hands are kept at one's sides or clasped in front or behind the body. The purpose is to slow down, be fully present in the moment, and become peaceful.

The first time Larry saw walking meditation was at a monastery. Far off in the distant horizon, five monks walked in unison, reminding him of five sailboats sailing smoothly and gracefully off into the sunset. His vision, as he described it to us, has stayed with me since.

Author Sarah Ban Breathnach, shares her own experience of walking as a meditation in her book *Simple Abundance*. One day she was so anxious she felt that she would jump out of her skin and bolted out of the house. "Filled with disappointments, painful memories, and my own expectations from the past—terrified of what the future held and changes that were inevitable—the only safe place for me was the present moment: my foot against the pavement, the wind on my face, my breath entering and leaving my body." Forty minutes later, she was amazed to find that she was calm and centered. Having made a habit of walking ever since, Sarah calls her moving meditation "fitness of the spirit."

Thich Nhat Hahn, a Vietnamese monk, author, and meditation teacher, tells us that "to have peace, you begin by walking peacefully." He teaches, "Breathing in, I know I'm breathing in. Breathing out, I know I'm breathing out . . . as we fill our lungs with air we are paying close attention to each step." We can connect with counting and say "in, in, in" with three steps and "out, out, out" with the next three steps, never controlling our breathing, always letting our breath be natural.

At first you might feel off-balance. That's all right. Soon your steps will smooth out as you begin to find your own rhythm. As little as ten minutes in this way can turn your day around from chaos to peace.

We can practice outside by being open and awake with all our senses. Being with the sky and the earth, the trees, flowers and birds, water, sand, or whatever else surrounds us, whatever we see, feel, hear, and touch.

While barely interrupting our busy schedule, we can make a simple choice to take a few minutes for walking meditation.

I am finding many opportunities to slow down, take time with myself, and be in the moment. As I give myself permission to take breaks in my hectic life, I am becoming centered and peaceful. ▓

Morning and Evening Prayer

I HAVE SO MUCH TO DO TODAY THAT I SHALL SPEND THE FIRST THREE HOURS IN PRAYER.

❧ MARTIN LUTHER (1483–1546)

What better way to start your day than by connecting with the energy and love of the God of your understanding. By simply having the intention to communicate with a power greater than yourself, your day begins on a positive and spiritual note. While most of us rarely have three hours to pray in the morning unless we are in a monastery, at a retreat, or on vacation, a few moments is all we need to ask for strength and guidance.

Many years ago, while still a doubter, a friend asked me, "If you were carrying a table and someone said they would help you by carrying one end, would you let her?" "Of course!" I answered. "Then why not let your Higher Power help you with your day?" continued my friend. Since then, because of count-less experiences of help I have received by inviting God into my day, my faith has deepened. I would not consider beginning my day without prayer. Now I simply ask for the knowledge of God's will for me and the power to carry it out. Madame Chiang Kai-Shek said that she used to pray that God would do this or that. Later she prayed that God would make His will known to her.

Imagine you are in a cold room with an electric heater at one end. If you plug the heater in and turn it on in the morning, you will be warm all day. The longer you wait, the colder the room gets. And if you wait until the end of the day, you would have spent a day being cold unnecessarily.

Morning prayer and meditation is, to me, a similar connec-tion with my higher self, my inner spirit, my Higher Power, God. I become willing to open myself up to the deepest place within me and to connect with all the energies of the universe, whatever they might be. I truly have no idea who or what God is, or whom or what I am praying to. But I do know that there is power and energy in the universe and when I pray, I make a connection to the power and energy.

Mahatma Gandhi tells us, "Prayer is the key of the morning and the bolt of the evening." Taking this time for ourselves, whether we take a few seconds or many minutes, doesn't matter. It is our quiet time, our personal time . . . our time for solitude.

The evening is a good time to thank this Higher Power for our day, perhaps giving specific thanks for some particular thing, event, or situation we experienced that day. Perhaps a prayer was answered or something went particularly well. Evening is a good time to review our day and, if need be, ask forgiveness for something we did that we are not proud of, perhaps some thoughtless or careless thing we did or said, a harm, an unintentional harm done to someone.

And then it is time to go to sleep, resting in the knowledge that you have done the best you could with this day.

Today I will take the time to pray, even if I don't know to whom I am praying. I will connect in the morning by asking and again in the evening by being grateful. I will know that the power I had during the day did not come solely from myself. 🎴

My Journey to Prayer

CERTAIN THOUGHTS ARE PRAYERS. THERE ARE MOMENTS WHEN, WHATEVER BE THE ATTITUDE OF THE BODY, THE SOUL IS ON ITS KNEES.

🍂 VICTOR HUGO

When I was young, I wanted a dog more than anything else in the entire world. Unfortunately, our landlords wouldn't allow animals and during World War II, my family lived in many different rented houses in Detroit, Michigan. Leases were signed for only one year at a time then so that the soldiers coming home from the war could be given priority in housing. As a result, we moved almost every year from the time I was two until I was ten, when we returned to Massachusetts.

With each new move I prayed that I would be able to have a dog. Each time it was the same story. The landlord said, "No dogs." My mother explained that we were lucky just to be able to rent a home.

Back then I had a habit that really bothered my mother. I twirled a piece of my hair over and over again. My mother constantly told me to stop, but I loved the way it felt. Finally I made a bargain with God. I prayed, "God, if you just let me have a puppy, I'll never twirl my hair again." Each time we moved, I pleaded to God to let me have a puppy. And each time, the same results. No dogs. No pets of any kind! I gave up praying for many years. God wouldn't answer me, so maybe there was no God.

By the time I went to college I was an agnostic. Maybe there was a God. Maybe there wasn't. I was convinced we would never know.

As the years went on, I started my own business, married, had three children, became a daily drinker, and gradually an alcoholic, no longer giving much thought as to whether or not there was a God. Eventually my drinking became such a problem I sought the help of a psychiatrist. During the next two years he overmedicated me with tranquilizers, antidepressants, and sleeping pills, thinking, mistakenly, that they would cure alcoholism. But, combining alcohol with prescription drugs, dangerous as it was, actually helped me hit bottom and I finally turned in desperation to a support group.

There, it was suggested that I ask for help from a power greater than myself. Not believing in God made prayer very difficult for me, but I knew I couldn't continue to live the way I was and that I could not stop drinking on my own.

My first prayer went like this, "God, if you're not there it doesn't matter and if you are, you'll understand, but please keep me away from a drink and a pill and a desire for a drink and a pill today." It worked! The miracle happened. I became a deeply grateful believer.

God is still a mystery to me, but my relationship with God has grown. I came to see God as a power for good and love. Keeping it very simple, I merely need to know there is a power greater than myself and that I am not in charge of the universe.

For me, God is energy, a force, a power for good and love to turn to in time of trouble and to thank often during the day. I agree with author, psychotherapist, and retreat leader Sylvia Boorstein who says that she likes prayers. She doesn't know what she's praying to or if she's praying to anything. She just likes praying.

I know I can connect with this a Power Greater Than Myself at any time, and that gives me great comfort.

The Power of Prayer and Meditation

GOD GRANT ME THE SERENITY TO ACCEPT THE THINGS I
CANNOT CHANGE, COURAGE TO CHANGE THE THINGS I CAN,
AND WISDOM TO KNOW THE DIFFERENCE.

Ann's father tried everything he could to save his business, including borrowing from his employee's pension fund. He had every intention of paying it back, but was picked up by the FBI and put in jail before he ever had the chance.

Ann was devastated. She loved her father dearly and knew she had no control over the situation. She and her family contacted their congressmen, trying everything they knew to free her father. In jail he had no way to pay back the money. To add to the family's pain, he was diagnosed with cancer soon after his arrest. There were days when Ann felt so heavy, so burdened, she thought her body would split in half.

Sitting still in solitude helped Ann to gain control of herself, the only thing she felt she could control. She meditated a few times a day for those ten long months. Soaking in a hot bath surrounded by candles soothed and relaxed her. She took long walks, even if it was freezing cold outside.

"It's just you and your Higher Power," she told me. "No one is going to fix it for me, no matter how much they love and care for me."

Author Sheldon Knopf tells us that no matter how well we are prepared, the moment belongs to God. We can do everything we know how to do and still not achieve the results we so deeply want. There are times when no matter how logically and reasonably we put out our truth, we may still be ignored. We cannot win.

When these painful times come, when life isn't fair and it feels as if it is too much to handle, when everything we do turns out to be ineffective in making a bad situation better, we can find peace, strength, and courage in solitude, prayer, and meditation. James Dillet Freeman wrote, "How far past speech the silence of a prayer can reach! We take the road of prayer and find it is the path to peace of mind."

In prayer we can let go of whatever is bothering us, trusting that God will let us know if there is something we can do. The anonymous author of *Each Day a New Beginning* tells us: "The magic is that when we loosen our grip on this day, this activity, this person, we get carried gently along and find that which we struggled to control happening smoothly and naturally."

Today I am turning over all my difficulties to a Power Greater than myself. I am taking time to be alone and quiet, finding comfort, courage and peace of mind as I pray to accept God's will. ▨

The Healing Power of Prayer

WE NEED TO FIND GOD AND GOD CANNOT BE FOUND IN NOISE AND RESTLESSNESS. GOD IS A FRIEND OF SILENCE. . . . THE MORE WE RECEIVE IN SILENT PRAYER, THE MORE WE CAN GIVE IN OUR ACTIVE LIFE. WE NEED SILENCE TO BE ABLE TO TOUCH SOULS.

❧ MOTHER TERESA

Susan has a peripheral vascular disease. Her arteries were blocked so her blood didn't go down to her legs. In February she began to feel pain in her right calf that quickly became intense. Nothing would alleviate the pain. On Memorial Day weekend she attended a retreat with her church and shared with them the pain she was experiencing. They added her to the church's prayer list and seventeen people began to pray for her daily. Within one week the level of her pain had dramatically dropped.

Thought is energy. Thought is transmitted. Prayer is a quiet communication with the God of your understanding. When many people pray for the same purpose or the same person, many believe that all that energy can make miracles happen. People even use telephone chains where one person calls two people, to call two people, and so on, to pray for a particular person. Today others are using e-mail to reach even more people. Requests often go out around the world for people to pray together at a specific time for world peace.

Scientific studies have proven that prayers aid healing. One recent study followed a group of cancer patients who were divided into three groups, one on medication, one on placebos, and one where individuals were prayed for regularly by family or friends or a church group. The group that people prayed for had a higher recovery rate than the other two groups.

We can pray in silence or aloud. Sometimes we may even shout at God in anger or in frustration. Praying with other people, such as in temples and churches or at sacred places like the wailing wall, is a time when we can feel we are in solitude even when surrounded. We can be part of a group and still have our own personal alone time with God.

We don't actually need silence or solitude to pray. Prayers take place amid the raging guns and bombs exploding in the battlefields of war or in the raging screams and pain exploding in the battlefields of our minds. We beg, implore, beseech, petition, bargain, plead, scream, and whisper to God in the most difficult times in our lives.

Prayers do not always give us the answers we seek. Nelia Gardner White advise us, "Some people just don't seem to realize when they're moaning about not getting prayers answered, that 'no' is the answer." When we seek the knowledge of God's Will for us and the power to carry it through, we get the courage and strength we need to get through whatever happens in our lives.

It is great comfort to know that there is a power greater than myself to turn to when I don't know what to do. ▓

Expanding Our State of Consciousness

I AM LARGER THAN I THOUGHT. I DID NOT KNOW I HELD SUCH GOODNESS.

— WALT WHITMAN

One morning while I was meditating, I became very aware that I was in a deep state of inner peace. My breathing had slowed down and I felt very centered and still. In this place of stillness I was aware that something else had also changed on the outside of my body. I'm sure it didn't look different, but my outer body felt softer. It also felt as if there was soft, peaceful space, perhaps a few inches wide that surrounded my body. The edges of my body seemed expanded and a part of that space.

I asked Katherine Baugh, an energy worker, what she thought happened to me. She told me that from her viewpoint, we are all light. She explained that my energy field had expanded. Perhaps I was in the flow of life, or connected to higher energy or connected to my Higher Power. Energetically, she said, we can be as big as we want to be. All religions tell us that we are part of God. Most of us feel disconnected and searching for "something," but we are not quite sure what. Some call that a spiritual longing or spiritual thirst or hunger.

I have read about this place before. Experiencing it and reading about it are entirely different things. Since clarifying that experience I am more aware that when I am tense, my entire body is tense, but I don't know this until I relax. Only in the process of relaxation can I feel my muscles soften and my breath slow down. When the "aha" time comes, the instant knowing and the letting go of the struggle, I release the tension I have been holding in a long breath. I can feel the tension pour out of me and I feel soft, gentle and the air surrounding my body supports this softening.

When we can let go of our "to-do" list and outside distractions we can simply be in the present moment. This offers us the opportunity to become aware of what is actually going on in any given moment. There are three levels. First there is the feeling. Then there is the awareness of the feeling. Then there is the awareness that we are aware of the feeling. For example, I experienced a deep sense of inner peace. I then became aware that the boundaries of my skin felt softer and somehow merged with the air around me. Then I became aware that I was aware of this extraordinary feeling. Most of the time we are experiencing life and reacting with feelings. Solitude opens the door for us to be aware of our experiences, our feelings, and our reactions to them. This leads to our really getting to know ourselves at a much deeper level.

Meditation is only one way of expanding our state of consciousness. Praying, visualizing, and guided imagery can bring us to this place. I have been told that fasting, chanting, drumming, dancing, running, and following a labyrinth can bring you there, too. It is a very spiritual state where one can feel connected with the entire universe. It is here that we find ourselves, the very essence of ourselves. We connect with our soul.

I am releasing all my tension, stress, and concerns as I bring my full attention to this very moment, getting with the flow of universal energy that is everywhere. ▦

ACTIVITIES
FOR PEACE AND
RENEWAL

*INSIDE MYSELF IS A PLACE WHERE I LIVE
ALONE AND THAT'S WHERE YOU RENEW
YOUR SPRINGS THAT NEVER DRY UP.* ✖

PEARL S. BUCK

Discover Silence

SILENCE IS A TOOL, A CONTEXT FOR DIRECT PERSONAL, INTUITIVE UNDERSTANDING OF HOW THINGS ARE. . . . ITS GREAT OVERRIDING VALUE IS THE SUPPORT IT PROVIDES FOR INSIGHT; ITS IMMEDIATE EVIDENCE IS, IT'S A RELIEF!

✤ SYLVIA BOORSTEIN

From the moment we wake up in the morning until the moment we fall asleep at night, our lives are almost always filled with noise. Our sleep is even filled with noise, although we aren't aware of it. There's a good chance that most of the sounds we hear around us come from many of the following: refrigerator motors, telephones, airplanes, radios, TVs, cars, trucks, doors slamming, door bells, water running, computers, printers, faxes, photocopy machines, dogs barking, children playing, answering machines, alarms, microwave buzzers, air conditioners, videos, and so much more! Depending on where you live there might be babies crying, trains whistling, backhoes roaring, or even saws whining. We become so conditioned to a great deal of this noise that we are barely aware of it. When is the last time that you were aware of your refrigerator's motor, for example? It's always on, but we usually become aware of it only when it stops. Only in the silence can we hear something missing.

Some of us are more sensitive to noise than others. I have a hard time when a clock is ticking, no matter how lightly. When I am away from home and hear a clock at night, I have to hide it under a cushion to fall asleep. But whether we consciously hear noise or not, it is there and we are far less serene when it is within our hearing range.

Take a machine noise break! Oliver Wendell Holmes, Sr., writes, "Silence comes to heal the blows of sound." It is wonderful just to be quiet and hear the birds or the waves, the barely audible sound of a grasshopper, or the rustle of leaves being lifted by the breeze. Silence heals us from the wounds of which we are barely aware. Take a walk into the woods and listen to the sounds of nature. Walk in a field of wild flowers or along the shore. Climb up a mountain or walk into a valley. Listen to the corn or palm leaves swaying.

If you can't leave the house, turn off the telephone and put your answering machine all the way down. Turn off the refrigerator for ten minutes. Don't turn on the TV, radio, or computer. Remove yourself from the sound of a ticking clock or any other repetitive noise. It can't do any harm and the silence will be amazingly peaceful.

Author Sylvia Boorstein calls silence the fence for wisdom. I love that image! I can see myself climbing over a fence from a place full of noise to a deliciously silent space where I effortlessly tune in to creativity and wisdom.

Mahatma Gandhi said that in the attitude of silence the soul finds the path in a clearer light. What is elusive and deceptive resolves itself into crystal clearness. He believed that our life is a long and arduous quest after truth.

If it is not possible to find time for silence during the day, wait for everyone to go to sleep, or wake up a few minutes before everyone else. Be with yourself in silence. A few moments of silence can start your day off with inner peace or end a hectic day with serenity.

Today I will nurture my soul by taking at least ten minutes to connect with the peace and tranquility of silence. ▓

A Change of Pace or Place

A CHANGE IS AS GOOD AS A REST.

✣ WINSTON CHURCHILL

Just the act of doing something differently, a change of pace or place, can be inspiring, stimulating, restful, and healing. We can feel dull when we do the same things over and over again. Not only does life become monotonous and boring, but our creativity is also stifled. We are kept from growing as women.

Routines certainly have their place. They're helpful to accomplish tasks. But routines can put us on automatic pilot, so that we respond in the same way over and over again. When I lived in my college dormitory many years ago, I remember being surprised at the different routines some classmates had. Some women washed their hair or did their laundry on the same day every week. I remember thinking how boring, to do the same thing every week! I saw myself as a creative person and I chose to be spontaneous and adventurous. Of course, my ironing was never done! And, I must admit, neither was some of my home-work. Discipline in the areas that were not interesting or stimulating to me was not one of my greatest assets.

Yet later, I discovered that to be creative I had to develop certain routines so that I would not be bogged down with details. When I traveled to speak at conferences or put on retreats and workshops, I was entirely organized. I traveled only with what I needed for that week, I had my clothes cleaned in time for packing. My hair was cut a week in advance so it would look its best for my presentation. My papers were always photocopied on time. My preparedness allowed me to be spontaneous and enthusiastic in my presentations because I wasn't worried about details.

On the other hand, if our lives are too disciplined by the same routines we can become bored. This can be true even for our precious gift of solitude. Perhaps your time for solitude has turned into a routine, rather than something you look forward to. Perhaps you are not finding the peace or joy you once felt when you took time for solitude. Maybe you're doing the same things over and over again. If so, you may find that a change of pace is good. You need to stimulate your creative juices to inspire you to try something different. Try to change the time of day you devote to solitude or, perhaps you can change the amount of time that you take for yourself.

Perhaps you take time for solitude with a daily walk. Vary your path. Walk at a different time. If you meditate by the ocean, try finding a place in the woods or by a lake. Use a different color pen for your journal writing. Try painting or sketching rather than writing your memoirs. Buy new gardening gloves in your favorite color. Extend the time you trade babysitting with your neighbor or friend. Make it two hours instead of one for a month. Hook a rug or get a yoga video. Go on a retreat.

Variety and change can spice up our lives and can give us fresh energy and renewed inspiration. Even solitude can become dull when it is taken at the same time and in the same way.

Today I will look at ways to vary my solitude, exploring new possibilities, perhaps even doing something I've never done before! ⚜

Clearing Out the Clutter

THE ANCIENT ART OF FENG SHUI AND SPACE CLEARING IS
TO CREATE A SACRED SPACE IN YOUR HOME OR WORKPLACE,
WHICH WILL ALLOW YOU TO CREATE MORE HEALTH, WEALTH
AND HAPPINESS IN YOUR LIFE.

❦ KAREN KINGSTON

Imagine turning on your faucet one day and seeing that the fresh clear water that usually pours out is flowing more slowly. Each day this flow slows down until it is nothing more than a trickle. Finally, it takes a plumber to clear the debris that has collected in the pipes, thus allowing the water to flow freely again.

Our energy is just like that water. When we have healthy energy, it flows easily. We feel good, we're healthy and happy. We attract positive people and good experiences into our lives. But when our energy is stuck, we're like the water in the clogged pipe, slow, tired, and perhaps even sick.

Metaphysics teachers tell us that clearing clutter releases huge amounts of energy. We lighten up in body, mind, and spirit. Katherine Ponder writes, "By letting go of the lesser, you are automatically making room for the greater good to come in."

When I'm writing or getting ready for a workshop or retreat, my papers and books are everywhere. But if I don't clean up after that project is complete, I find it difficult to go on to something new. I have struggled with clutter all my life. What works best for me is to stop and take the time to put away everything I am not working on in that present moment.

Feng Shui is the art of balancing, harmonizing, and enhancing the flow of natural energies. It has become very popular in the United States lately, although it has been well known in the East for more than three-thousand years. Space Clearing is the art of cleansing and consecrating spaces.

There is a life force or energy in everything. The word *feng* means wind. The word *shui* means water. The Chinese use the word *chi* for our life force, the interconnection to all that is in the universe. The Japanese call it *Ki*, the Hindus call it *prana,* and in America we call it *spirit*, *life force,* or *energy*.

Karen Kingston, author of *Creating Sacred Space with Feng Shui,* suggests that what is in your outer life is in your inner self. She believes that when you are stuck on some problem in your life, there is always a corresponding stuckness in some part of your home. She writes, "By clearing the energy in your home, and getting it moving again, the problem starts to resolve. Revitalizing the atmospheres around you has a corresponding effect on your energy."

Karen goes on to say that when we keep objects "just in case" we need them, we're telling our subconscious mind we're preparing for a situation of neediness in the future. We're sending a message to the universe that we don't trust it to provide for us and that we'll always be vulnerable and insecure about the future.

If you want new things in your life, get rid of the old. Clear out your bureau drawers and closets. Give your clothes away to a halfway house or a shelter where they are needed.

As you take more and more time for yourself in solitude, you will become more in touch with your own energy. You'll learn to trust what makes you feel good and what drains and depletes your energy. Take time to walk slowly through your house and see what you don't use anymore and what pulls down your energy. Let go of whatever doesn't fill you with good feelings.

By letting go of all that is no longer important in my life, I can make space for something new and fresh. I can be open to new thoughts and ideas when I am not being held back by old and useless things. ▨

If God Would Speak to Me

BE STILL AND KNOW THAT I AM GOD.

PSALM 46:10

I do some of my best thinking on airplanes. I often take my laptop computer and words fly from my mind to my fingers to my keyboard. Most likely it's because I can be very single-focused on a plane. There is no phone to interrupt, no deadline to make, no clutter around me. I have only what I need with me, and I just let the pilot do all the work. It is a wonderful time for solitude. I stay in my seat, rarely talk to anyone, and luxuriate in my own private, uninterrupted world.

Years ago, while on a plane heading to Peoria, Illinois, I realized how very tired I was. I had recently conducted a series of workshops and retreats and my latest book was not selling as fast as I wished. I was discouraged. Suddenly an idea came to me. If God would speak to me, what would God say?

I knew the value of opposite handwriting. So, with my dominant hand I wrote, "If You would speak to me, God, what would You say?" And to my surprise, this is what poured out of me from my opposite hand:

> *"Good Morning, Ruth,*
> *I really am real! I really am here . . . and here for you!*
> *You have worked for a long time and you are very,*
> *very tired. You have tried your best to serve me and to*
> *be a good person. You have tried very, very hard. You*
> *have worked very, very hard. And I am grateful. I see*
> *your efforts. I have watched your efforts. I acknowl-*
> *edge your efforts. Relax now. Let Me help you. Let*

Me make your life easier. Believe that I can do this for you and it will happen. Believe in Me and I will be there for you. Believe in Me. Trust Me. You will see a difference in your life. No more efforting. Go with the flow. Take all that you have learned . . . and know it is real. Relax. Trust. Feel My Love for you. You are lovable and I love you. I bless you.

Tears flowed softly when I finished, as feelings of love and relief poured over me. There was no question for me that I had experienced a spiritual connection.

Writing to your Higher Power with your nondominant hand is a wonderful exercise for gaining insight into a situation or making a deeper connection to your soul. Take time when you won't be interrupted. Unplug all telephones within hearing or put the answering machine on low. Either go some place where you can be alone or hang a "Do Not Disturb" sign on your door.

Begin with a few minutes of meditation, prayer, or quiet breathing. When you feel centered and spiritually connected, write on the top of a clean sheet of paper with your dominant hand: "If You would speak to me, God, what would You say?" (Use any word you are comfortable with here, such as Higher Power, Spirit, etc.).

Write the answer with your opposite hand. This may seemed awkward or forced at first. If words don't come, put this idea aside for another time. Use any of these exercises only when they feel comfortable.

When the time is right, I will quietly connect with my Higher Power. I will write down my questions and trust the answers I receive in prayer and meditation. ▦

It's Time for Fun!

ALL WORK AND NO PLAY MAKES JANE A DULL GIRL.

❧ OLD MAXIM

One Sunday I found myself far behind in my work, but I was determined to take the day off. My mind had other ideas and didn't want me to stop. It reminded me continually of all the work piled up on my desk and all the deadlines in the coming week. Try as I might to ignore them, the papers in my office kept calling to me, but I knew my mind needed a rest.

It was cold and damp outside, threatening to rain at any moment. I had planned to work in the garden, but it was too dreary. A few years earlier I had bought two unpainted bird houses and had never got around to decorating them. The interest just wasn't there, but on this Sunday I took out the paints and brushes and began to paint. Before long I became aware of a quiet, peaceful state of mind that I had not felt since my morning meditation, a sense of personal accomplishment and connectedness. The papers in my office were silent and my mind was quiet at last!

There are so many things we can do in solitude. It takes just a few minutes to trick our minds into leaving the ruts of repetitive thinking and move into a creative activity. Elizabeth Ladd advises us that if we enjoy our own company, we'll never be lonely. Find the things you like doing so you can enjoy your own company. They can be active or inactive activities. Knitting, crossword puzzles, gardening, fishing, walking, writing, and painting are just a few of the many things we can do quietly and alone. Cooking, canning, or playing a musical instrument, cross country skiing, and horseback riding are a few more.

Exploring the Internet can be peaceful. It can take us from one place to another to another, very quickly. In no time at all we can find ourselves in different world. But do be careful because the Internet can also be very addictive. A recent poll showed that those who spend a long time alone on the Internet can develop mild depression.

Sit down with a good book or write a book! Repot overgrown plants and decorate their containers. Learn a new hobby. Take all your pictures that you have been collecting over the years and put them in albums. Or create a collage of your trips or special outings. Sew a quilt or knit a sweater. You're only limited by your imagination. Is it time to put some new activities into your life?

Today I am finding something special I like to do and I'm making the time to do it . . . no matter what! ❖

The Sounds of Life

YES IN JOY YOU SHALL DEPART, IN PEACE YOU SHALL BE BROUGHT BACK; MOUNTAINS AND HILLS SHALL BREAK OUT IN SONG BEFORE YOU, AND ALL THE TREES OF THE COUNTRYSIDE SHALL CLAP THEIR HANDS.

❧ ISAIAH, 55:12

The world is alive with sounds and we're usually too busy to hear them. Often we are so caught up in the everyday details of our lives that even to consider slowing down and simply listening is not high on our "to-do" list.

Do it anyway! Some day take some time to stop. Be still. Listen. What do you hear? Perhaps cars and trucks outside? Maybe an airplane is passing overhead. Can you hear your breath as it comes in and goes out? How about birds chirping, the pages of your book as you turn them or your shoes as they land on the ground, one by one? Tune in to your own sniffing, yawning, scratching, sighing—all the sounds we make naturally without noticing.

A very wise person once wrote: "Have you ever watched kids on a merry-go-round, or listened to rain slapping the ground? Ever followed a butterfly's erratic flight, or gazed at the sun fading into the night? You better slow down, don't dance so fast, time is short, the music won't last."

Next time you are out of doors, listen. What can you hear? The sounds of water or waves, leaves or snow crunching under your feet, or acorns falling? Maybe you can hear the soft sound of sand falling through your fingers, the crunch of a shovel digging into the earth, a fly or a bee buzzing by, maybe a squirrel swishing its tail.

A high school teacher told me that in warm weather she takes her classes outside. The students are asked to close their eyes, pretend they are blind, and tune in to all their other senses. They are asked to move around, smell the flowers and the grass, use their hands to get in touch with their sense of touch, feel the breeze on their faces, and listen to all the sounds around them. Try this sometime. It's very powerful.

Author Pema Chodron tells us "The sky and the sun are always there, it's the storms and the clouds that come and go." Our own storms of busyness, fear of saying no and thus being rejected, or being overwhelmed with unimportant details that can wait until tomorrow keep us from being present to the sounds of life. Stopping and listening slow us down and bring peace to the moment.

We could go on and on. Have your own listening experience. If you wonder why you should bother, know that it truly brings you into the moment. It awakens your senses and helps you feel more alive. You become more aware of your sense of touch, smell, taste, and sight. You might notice how your own body feels more alive. You can feel more connected to the universe.

I am giving myself the gift of slowing down to listen closely to the sounds of life around me, I can feel the joy of being fully alive in each moment. 🎴

Exploring Our Spirituality

The degree of harmony that comes into your experience is proportionate to the degree of your own spiritual development.

🐚 Joel Goldsmith

At the time when I was just beginning to recover from alcoholism, I didn't believe in God. I knew there had to be "something" because I didn't drink when I prayed to this "Power Greater than myself." I saw other people staying sober and happily helping others. Many hadn't picked up a drink or a drug for years. I had to admit there must be "something out there" when I contemplated the changing of the season, the turning of the tides, the rising and setting of the sun.

Someone helped me by suggesting that I add a letter "O" into the word God and think of God as "good." Someone else suggested that I think of God as love. I could accept this. God is "good" and God is "love." We all have our own personal understanding of God.

We receive our earliest lessons from our family and religious training. As we mature, many of us leave the religion we were born into and struggle to find our own answers. Some of us return to our early faith while others join another religion. Still others continue on a different and personal spiritual path, never rejoining any religion at all. Spirituality is such a individual process!

Solitude is a wonderful place to spend time contemplating what you believe. For example, why not think about what has changed for you on your own spiritual path. Read some books and listen to inspirational tapes. Take a course in spirituality. Perhaps you could attend a church or a synagogue and explore what those experiences mean to you.

Look at the positive and negative influences that have affected what you believe today. Consider whether you are happy with your relationship, or lack of relationship, with a Higher Power in your life today? Ask yourself if there is something missing in your spiritual life. Question if you feel connected and whole.

I'm taking time to explore my own relationship with God. Praying, meditating, reading, and thinking are all ways that I can deepen my understanding and come to my own truth. ✳

Out of Our Minds!

BE OUT OF YOUR MIND!

❧ CAROL DUBIN

When I was a young child, I remember lying in bed at night for hours, unable to fall asleep. My mind was so active it wouldn't stop. I recall thinking "I have to stop thinking." Then I would think, "I have to stop thinking that I'm thinking." And then, "I have to stop thinking that I'm thinking that I'm thinking!" And on and on I would go with this. I had a clue then about what I later considered my craziness. My mind could make me feel crazy.

It was not until years later that I learned that I was not the only one who had this experience. Once I started talking about it, I learned that most people had times when they felt that if their minds didn't stop thinking they, too, would go crazy. I wasn't so unusual after all!

Later, I began to learn more about stress. I learned that our stress comes from what we do with our thoughts and how we react to what is going on in our lives. I learned that we didn't have to go around and around in our thinking like a hamster on a wheel. We could actually stop our repetitive thinking and change our negative thought patterns. What a relief it is to know that we are not prisoners of our minds!

At a recent workshop, Carol Dubin, a yoga teacher, spoke of the value of yoga and how it gets us "out of our minds" and into our bodies. She joked that being out of our minds is a good thing. She said, "Be out of your mind. Just be with your experience."

When you feel as if you are about to explode from stress or obsessive thinking, take some time for yourself! Meditate. Become aware of your breath as it goes in and comes out of your nose. Take one minute and see how many times you do breathe in and out in a minute. Practice some yoga exercises. Get in touch with your body as it pulls and stretches. Take a walk and feel the muscles in your legs and the swing of your arms. Lie down and feel your body pressing against the rug or the floor. Mentally scan over your body, bringing your attention to your entire body from the top of your head down to the bottom of your feet.

These are just a few ways we can take time to release stress and stop the endless chatter that goes on in our minds. Simply by bringing our attention to our bodies, we can achieve instant relief. The peace we experience will stay with us long after we have returned to our daily activities.

It is great to be out of my mind! I am continuing to explore new ways to stop the clutter and worry that go on in my mind by simply bringing my attention to my body. ▨

Excuse Box

PEACE CAN ONLY EXIST IN THE PRESENT MOMENT. IT IS RIDICULOUS TO SAY, "WAIT UNTIL I FINISH THIS, THEN I WILL BE FREE TO LIVE IN PEACE."

❧ THICH NHAT HANH

How often have you said to yourself, "I'll take some time for me after I. . . ." The blank could be: the kids are older, when I get a baby sitter, when I finish a project, school, etc., etc., etc. It is easy to put off your own needs because of the many things that can fill up your life. Some of us are so used to doing for others, it is hard even to think of taking time for ourselves when someone else needs us, or we think they need us. Design an excuse box for yourself! It can be any box at all, new or used. Write or paint the word "excuses" on it. Design it any way you want so that it will be yours and you will feel good about it.

Whenever you hear yourself saying, "I'll take some time for me after I . . . ," listen closely to what you are saying and write it down on a piece of paper. Don't justify it by telling yourself it is true. Know it is simply an excuse and put the paper in your excuse box. Then, every time you think of the excuse that's keeping you from enjoying your special time, which you really do deserve, know that you have put that in the excuse box. You've turned it over to all the energies of the universe. Know that through your willingness and openness, positive solutions will appear. Time will open up for you in ways you could never have imagined.

Today I am letting go of all the excuses that keep me from taking that precious time for me. I am putting my excuses in my excuse box, trusting that free time is coming my way! ✺

Reading

THERE IS NO FRIGATE LIKE A BOOK
TO TAKE US LANDS AWAY.

EMILY DICKINSON

I love to read. Each time I read a new inspirational, self-help, or spiritual book I hope for a new insight, a new answer to make my life easier. I think "At last! I'm going to learn the secret, the answer, find the truth that I have been missing all these years." I underline and take notes, finding "aha's!" and think Yes! This is it! And it is it, for the moment, until I put the book down and continue with life as it really is. But sometime in the future while I am in the midst of some struggle or stress, I remember a special line or thought from something I have read and it helps me through the moment.

The beach is one of my favorite places to read. They say you can't do two things at once but at the beach I can be lost in a book and get a tan at the same time!

Whether we are reading with our back supported by a friendly tree in the woods or against a cool rock beside a quiet stream; whether we are cushioned by the pillow of our own bed, or bouncing along on a crowded streetcar, reading can be a wonderful companion for solitude.

It doesn't matter whether we're drawn to mystery, self-help, inspiration, poetry, or novels. Just to be able to relax with any book is a gift we can give ourselves. It can stir the imagination and take us off to far-away places. It can be a welcome relief from our day-to-day concerns and routines. Reading can be our teacher and our friend. Kathleen Norris, author of *Hands Full of Living*, wrote "Just the knowledge that a good book is waiting at the end of a long day makes that day happier."

I always plan to keep a book on hand for the moment when I want to escape. It can take me into the world of solitude and relaxation, even when I am in a crowd. ▦

Connections

THE SOURCE OF LOVE IS DEEP IN US, AND WE CAN HELP OTHERS REALIZE A LOT OF HAPPINESS. ONE WORD, ONE ACTION, ONE THOUGHT CAN REDUCE ANOTHER PERSON'S SUFFERING AND BRING THAT PERSON JOY.

❧ THICH NHAT HANH

As I was sealing an envelope with an invoice in it one day, I realized that I hadn't included an inspirational poem for Martha who would okay the bill. I was disturbed because I usually included one when mailing the invoice and knew she appreciated them. I considered opening the envelop to include it. Was I being too compulsive or obsessive? My partner walked into my office at that moment and I shared my struggle. She laughed and kiddingly said that maybe Martha will think I didn't like her anymore if I didn't include it.

For other people I don't know, I often print little cards with the message, "Have a beautiful and peaceful day" and include them when I pay my bills. It makes me feel good when I do things like this. I can picture some woman working in the billing department of a large company opening envelope after envelope all day long and all she sees are checks and bill stubs. It must be so boring! And then she opens mine and the little message falls out, bringing a smile to her face. I smile, too, just imagining the scene.

So here I was with the mild dilemma, hardly worth giving it this much thought. I didn't want Martha to think I don't care about her. I carefully opened the sealed envelope, printed out an inspirational saying from the hundreds I have stored on my computer, folded the paper, enclosed it, and resealed the envelope with scotch tape. I felt better, glad I had taken the time.

I began to think more about connection. The idea of sending just an invoice to a friend, a person who is more than just a stranger, felt cold. A friend once told me he stops his work early every Friday around 4:00 P.M. and spends the next hour connecting, either by phone or mail, with someone he hasn't seen in a while. I always thought that was such a heart-warming idea.

Connection can be an important part of solitude. We need time alone and time to connect. To be a whole person, we need to feel a "part of." We need community.

We might choose to write a letter to a friend we haven't seen in a long time or just catch up on some correspondence when we are taking time for solitude. We can buy birthday and anniversary cards early and write them out ahead of time so that they will be ready to mail at the appropriate time. This is a great way to stay in touch with the people you care about.

A newsletter is another great way to stay connected. Take some of your alone time and write about the highlights of your life. You can send it out in place of holiday cards or you can send it out whenever you feel like it for no reason at all.

Solitude is a wonderful time to connect with people we care about in our minds and in our hearts while still enjoying the peace and quiet of being away from the hectic activities of everyday life.

Thinking of my friends and family and making a connection with them expand my heart and let more love in. Today I will think of at least one way to expand my heart as I connect with others. 🦋

Personal Retreats

IN THE ATTITUDE OF SILENCE THE SOUL FINDS THE PATH IN A CLEARER LIGHT, AND WHAT IS ELUSIVE AND DECEPTIVE RESOLVES ITSELF INTO CRYSTAL CLEARNESS. OUR LIFE IS A LONG AND ARDUOUS QUEST AFTER TRUTH.

MAHATMA GANDHI

Dr. Gina Ogden, author and psychotherapist, who was healing from a very intense knee surgery, knew she had to get away by herself. Although both before and after her surgery, Gina received tremendous support from her partner and friends, at some point she began fantasizing about a cabin in the woods and felt compelled to find one. She found it at a conference center only two and a half hours away from her home and she reserved it immediately.

Gina had been neglected as a child and she still suffers from fear of abandonment and of being alone. Therefore, this desire for solitude surprised her, but she decided to trust her inner urging. She brought with her a bag of brown rice, carrots, vitamin pills, and oatmeal. She also had her laptop computer, a drum, stones to make runes, a pendulum, and meditation tapes. She took off her watch, not wanting to be bound by time.

Once settled in, it took her two days to adjust to the realization of being really alone. She set up candles and made a space for meditation. She became aware of rain and stopped everything, listening to the sound and smell of rain landing in the woods. When a thunderstorm came up, she took great joy in noticing what happened when the rain hit the leaves and ground.

She slept an enormous amount of time during the first week. After a few days she wasn't even hungry. She loved the idea that she could be naked all day if she wanted to be. At first she did a lot of body movement, and meditated. She made of labyrinth of sacred geometry. By the second week this was too much work. She had totally unstructured time, just asking herself what she wanted to do next. Sometimes she decided she just didn't want to do anything.

Five days before it was time to leave, Gina began getting back into her own rhythm and felt ready to return home.

Many things changed for Gina as a result of this experience. Her relationship with the telephone and mail was different. She stopped reading catalogues. E-mail messages made her crazy. She began to simplify her life.

Gail is a nurse in a very busy doctor's office with barely a minute for herself in any given day. Five years ago, she decided to take a trip to Florida and stay in a motel by herself. She rented a bike rather than a car, so she had to bike or walk everywhere. The television set was never turned on, but she had brought lots of books with her.

At first she was nervous about this adventure. Friends couldn't understand why she was going alone. However, she enjoyed the silence and time for herself so much that she has repeated her personal retreat annually for the last five years. She looks forward to it with each passing year.

These are just two examples of personal retreats. Some women go to the woods, mountains, the ocean, or the desert and set up a tent. You can live on a boat, in a camper, or recreational vehicle. Or, you can stay at home, turning off everything that makes noise, including the telephone, and not answering the door bell.

My need for solitude can be met only by following my internal motivation. I am listening to my inner spirit to tell me when the time is right. ▓

Gratitude List

*SO THE RISING SUN IS REASON ENOUGH FOR THANKFUL-
NESS, IN THAT ANOTHER DAY HAS COME. LET US SEE THE
BEAUTY IN OURSELVES AND ONE ANOTHER.*

         DHYANI YWAHOO

One day in October, while teaching meditation to the women at Barnstable County House of Corrections, one woman asked me if the leaves outside had started to change. "Will I see them when I get out? Will they still be there by October 24?" Her eyes filled with tears.

The impact of what she had said didn't hit me until later, when I walked back to my car. Here I was, a free woman, walking to my car. I was free to drive my car to my house and do what I wanted to do for the rest of the day. I had the freedom to watch the trees change color and to know that I would be able to watch them fall and see them bud again in the spring.

My eyes filled with tears, both for the pain that woman was going through and for the gratitude I felt in my heart. Until that moment I had taken my freedom for granted. It was a wake up call for me to be more aware of all the things I had to be grateful for in my life.

No matter how dark life can seem at times, when we take time to find something to be grateful for, we won't be pulled down into despair and depression. Gratitude lists are wonderful to keep because when life does feel as if it offers us nothing but trouble our list can remind us of the things we have for which we are grateful, even though we can't think of one on our own at the time.

Meister Eckhart wrote the wise words, "If the only prayer you said in your whole life was, 'thank you,' that would be enough."

Today I am thinking about all the things I have to be grateful for and will write them down. I will make a gratitude list, adding to it every time I think of something new. By doing this I will be more aware of the things I have to be grateful for and will always have something about which I can feel good, no matter what is going on in my life. ▩

The Healing Power of Journaling

JOURNAL KEEPING REQUIRES COURAGE AND SWEATERS. COURAGE BECAUSE IT'S OFTEN HARD AND PAINFUL TO SEE YOUR LIFE BEFORE YOU IN BLACK AND WHITE; SWEATERS BECAUSE WE ALL NEED SOMETHING TO COZY UP TO.

❧ RICHARD SOLLY

Journaling is a very special and intimate time we take for ourselves. I have frequently turned to my journal over the years as a vehicle to express what was going on in my life. Sometimes I've used it to record significant events, but most often I have journaled to help me through difficult times. My journal carries me from one place to another, moves me, helps me to become unstuck. At various times it has served as a bridge, allowing me to leave my pain behind so that I could move on; and it has been a safe container for my feelings.

Years ago I bought a leather journal cover and a beautifully bound book with blank pages to put inside it. My intention was to write everyday. I thought of it as my formal journal and planned to use it for all the momentous occasions I wanted to remember, times I went through a great deal of pain or confusion, or when I was in the midst of a heavy decision or change. It became a regular part of my life.

It was very special. I held it very gently and with great respect. I honored it as if it were sacred. I knew it held my deepest truth and sincerity, my dreams and disappointments, my sorrows and my struggles.

I reached for it in the days after my son died. Looking back later through my journal, I cannot believe the intensity of the pain I felt at that time of my life. I came to understand that I was writing words I was incapable of saying aloud. It served to clear the massive, uninvited, intrusive, and heavy burden that stuck inside my gut and my chest and my throat. Putting words to the horror that I was feeling served to move around the energy of the pain so that it could be released and I could be free to go through the motions of doing whatever was required of me each day. Some days the words just poured out while other days I just stared at the paper without any words at all and I simply wrote a few words such as, "terrible day,"or "Here I go again." I knew instinctively the natural inclination of my soul and followed it. My journal was a safe place to turn, a trusted friend. It gave me great comfort and was a wonderful release.

I was fortunate enough to know that whatever was going on inside me needed to be expressed to the outside or it would damage me mentally, physically, and spiritually. At another level, the writer part of me also knew that when I became ready to share it with others, it would help them, too.

To express how we feel, whether to another person or to the pages of our journal, helps us along the path of healing. Let the words and feelings come out without concern for grammar or form or even for making any sense. Let these pages serve as a safe container for your thoughts and feelings. You never have to share these words with anyone. It is up to you.

I am willing to express all the feelings that have been holding me back from living the joyous and authentic life I was meant to live. I can search deep within me and write them down in my journal, knowing every step takes me closer to healing and freedom. ✺

Many Forms of Journaling

BE A DOLPHIN. DIVE DEEP AND SURFACE. GO INTO THE HEART OF THE ISSUE, THEN COME SHARPLY TO THE SURFACE, LOOK AROUND, GRAB SOME AIR, GO BACK INTO THE HEART.

✤ KATHLEEN ADAMS

There are many forms of journaling. You can record your life story as it is happening, creating a record of your life history. You can check in daily and jot down what you are feeling in the moment, or write about the highlights of your day. You can write about a specific situation, a significant event, or a decision you might be struggling with at the time.

Journaling has great value for us as we look back to the past as well as while we are expressing and releasing our feelings in the present. We begin to see our life as it flows and moves, observing how it never stands still. Elbert Hubbard writes that

"The cure for grief is motion." Journaling can be just the motion we need to move us through any unresolved grief. Journaling helps us to maintain a perspective in our life in the midst of movement and change. We can look at where we are stuck and where we repeat patterns that get us in trouble.

Free flow writing lets us pour out our feelings. Many women have said when they do this in the morning they find increased energy for the rest of the day.

In the fourth step of Alcoholics Anonymous it is suggested that we do a searching and fearless moral inventory of the exact nature of our wrongs. This is a step in personal housekeeping, a way of looking deeply into the patterns that have gotten us in trouble or caused us difficulty. We list all our resentments, examine the cause of them and how they may affect us today.

The book *Alcoholics Anonymous* teaches its members to make a "strenuous effort to face, and to be rid of, the things in ourselves that have been blocking us. . . . Nothing counted but thoroughness and honesty." We do not need to be members of a twelve-step program to benefit from this practice.

Journaling can be helpful to understand where we are right now, By asking ourselves questions such as:

Where am I now?
What led up to where I am now?
What do I wish to learn from today?
Is there something in my life I wish to change?
To change, I must be willing to let go of:
My fears around letting go of this are:
Is there something I have to let go of?

There are other great values of journaling. It slows us down, for one thing. The act of picking up a pen or pencil, placing it on the page, and transferring the thoughts that are in our minds to that piece of paper places us directly in the present moment. We can feel the pen and the paper, hear their sounds, smell their uniqueness. Our minds are focused instead of racing off into other directions.

Yet journaling does not always have to be written by hand in a notebook. I have found that when I am short of time or filled with what feels like a million things to say, I turn on the computer where I can write faster and let it flow, whatever I'm feeling, whatever is coming up for me. It's a wonderful release and a way to get clarity in a time of confusion.

It's exciting to know I have so many choices that help me to grow, to be free, to move on. ✻

Preparing to Write

FIND YOUR OWN QUIET CENTRE OF LIFE, AND WRITE FROM THAT TO THE WORLD.

✻ SARAH ORNE JEWETT

Journaling is a very private and personal experience that will probably feel different from day to day, year to year. There are times when I can't wait to begin writing in my journal. Words bubble up inside of me, eager to pour out. As soon as my pen touches the paper, my pen flows nonstop until whatever it was that had been going on deep within me has expressed itself completely. It doesn't matter where I am, in my bedroom, my office, or even in my car when my feelings are that close to the surface.

Other times, each word can be a struggle because I'm not quite sure what I am feeling and it takes a while to get started.

Here are a few ideas that may help make journal writing a smooth and comfortable experience.

We need to find a place where we feel safe, a quiet space far enough away from everyone so that there are no interruptions. Whenever possible, it is better to have abundant time, so as not to feel rushed.

We can do many things to create our own personal space. For example:

> Light a candle or many candles
> Play mood music
> Have a favorite stuffed animal nearby
> Have a pet with you for company
> Burn incense
> Have plenty of paper and pens or pencils on hand
> Ask the family or whomever you live with for privacy
> Turn the ringer off on your phone and put the answering machine on low
> Put a DO NOT DISTURB SIGN on the door
> Use a book or notebook that feels good to you and keep it in a safe place.
> Write a focusing statement such as: I know my Higher Power is with me as I write

Kathleen Adams in her book *The Way of the Journal: A Journal Therapy Workbook for Healing* suggests that we put on the front page of our journal:

STOP! THIS IS THE
PERSONAL JOURNAL OF:

DO NOT READ ANY
FURTHER UNLESS YOU HAVE BEEN
GIVEN PERMISSION

She also suggests that we write the word *breathe* at the top of every page and stop writing when we feel overwhelmed.

Kathleen has a few good ways to get started. One is called Warm-ups, made up of the beginning of sentences you can finish with the first words that come to your mind, without censoring or judgments, such as:

> Right now I feel...
> If I had the time I would...
> My inner critic says I'm...
> My inner wisdom says I'm...
> If my present mood were a color it would be...

Remember this is for you alone and never has to be shared with anyone. Write only what you are comfortable putting on paper.

It can be helpful to begin with a meditation to find a quiet place within you. Begin quietly by listening to your breath as it comes in and goes out of your nose. Get in touch with your feelings. Let your thoughts go as they connect with your feelings. Don't pay any special attention to anything. Let yourself go to a very special place where you feel safe inside. Invite your Higher Power, God, or Spirit in and let yourself feel the safety and peace of this moment. Sit quietly for a few moments until you feel calm and relaxed.

I know I can experiment with a number of ways to get in touch with the deepest part of me. My Higher Power is guiding me to the best way for me today.

Letter Writing

THE DOORS WE OPEN AND CLOSE TODAY DECIDE THE LIVES WE LIVE.

FLORA WHITTEMORE

Many years ago I had a deep fear of my father. He had been physically abusive only once to me when I was very little, but the threat of abuse was always there. When he drank he became very loud and angry. His face became red, and he shook a threatening fist at anyone who disagreed with him.

When my children were little, he would take them for drives. His drinking worried me, but I knew he wouldn't listen if I tried to talk to him about it. One day I got the courage to write him a letter. I wrote, "Please don't drive the kids when you have been drinking." He answered, "Don't ever talk to me like that again."

I was not proud of the fact that I didn't have the courage to confront him. But I felt better when I expressed myself in the only way I could at that time. It took me many more years to learn to speak up to him.

Writing letters is a powerful technique for expressing and releasing negative and destructive feelings. For example, if you are very angry at someone who has hurt you, express all your anger in a letter. Say everything you wouldn't say face to face. Get it all out. It is important when you are doing this to know that it is an exercise to become free in this moment. You might never send the letter at all, but write it as if you are sending it. Put it away for at least twenty-four hours. Then you can decide to tone it down, send it as is, or not send it at all.

Letter writing works well for forgiveness also. You might have hurt someone intentionally or unintentionally. It might feel too threatening to face that person directly. To be free of the guilt you are carrying, write a letter expressing your amends. Again, hold this letter for twenty-four hours and then make a decision as to whether or not you want to mail it. You might decide that you do want to meet with this person face to face or just use the letter to express yourself.

Asking forgiveness by letter is most helpful if someone you have hurt has died and you are still carrying the feelings of guilt and shame. Write a sincere letter as if your are truly writing to this person. The key here is that you would be willing to make amends if it were possible.

Today I can empty myself of all anger and resentments so that I can let love come into my heart. ✻

The Power of Affirmations

THOUGHTS OF YOUR MIND HAVE MADE YOU WHAT YOU ARE AND THOUGHTS OF YOUR MIND WILL MAKE YOU WHAT YOU BECOME FROM THIS DAY FORWARD.

✻ CATHERINE PONDER

When my first book *The Journey Within: A Spiritual Path to Recovery,* was printed, my publisher called to ask if I did public speaking. I said no. He asked if I would consider it and I said no. He asked if I would call him back in two weeks and I didn't. I was terrified of public speaking! I had some very embarrassing times as a child in school and vowed I would never speak in front of people again. Peter called back in three weeks and told me I was on the agenda to speak in Albany, New York, in October, three months away. Three months to be nervous!

After listening to my negative self-talk such as "I'm not good enough," and "Who would want to hear me speak?" for over two months, I remembered, fortunately, that affirmations work. I teach my students to write affirmations ten times a day for twenty-one days. I only had nineteen days left before the conference, but I still wrote the following affirmation ten times a day for nineteen days, hoping it would be enough time for it to work: "I am a dynamite, confident, fearless, charismatic, and motivating speaker." I didn't believe one word of it and was embarrassed to tell anyone, but the power of those words carried me through that engagement and many others until I have finally become relaxed and even enjoy speaking.

As we take time for solitude, we learn to quiet our minds and listen to our self-talk, the words we tell ourselves. We begin to see these words have the power to make us feel good or bad, confident or fearful, positive or negative. It has been scientifically proven that the words we tell ourselves can even make us healthy or sick.

Once we realize that how we feel is a direct result of how we talk to ourselves, then we have a new and powerful tool to change how we feel. We have a choice. Affirmations are powerful tools to help us to break away from our past messages. By changing our thinking we can change our attitude, which helps us to change our actions, so we can change our lives.

Affirmations are so simple that many people think they are too simple to work. I have used them and have taught them to hundreds of people and the results have been amazing.

Shakti Gawain, author of *Creative Visualization,* wrote that when completing an affirmation, know or say, "This or something better for all concerned is manifesting itself for me." It is not always true that we know what is best for ourselves, and if we learn to wait and listen, the right answer will be there.

Affirmations must be:

1. *Positive.* Say "I am confident today," not "I am no longer negative."
2. Said and felt with *Passion* and *Power.* "I am CONFIDENT today!"
3. Keep in the *Present* moment. Say, "I am confident *TODAY*," not "I will be confident."
4. *Possible.* I could not affirm that I am a famous singer as I am tone deaf; but I could affirm that I am a successful writer.
5. *Personal.* We cannot affirm for someone else, only ourselves.

Try it for twenty-one days and witness for yourself the miraculous changes that happen in your life. If you miss a day in the series, you must start over again for it to be effective.

I have all the time I need to take time for me today. ✳

Personal Affirmations

WHAT WE CREATE WITHIN IS ALWAYS MIRRORED OUTSIDE OF US. THAT IS THE LAW OF THE UNIVERSE.

❧ SHAKTI GAWAIN

I received a call from a young woman who had attended one of my workshops. She told the following story: She had been out of control with her spending and had been too afraid to tell anyone. Purchases were hidden under her bed, never looked at once they were home. Closets were full of new, unworn clothes. If she were depressed or upset, or felt anything she didn't want to feel, shopping gave her the adrenaline rush she needed, or thought she needed, to get through the rough time, to lift her mood. She was close to deep financial trouble and she was physically sick with worry and shame.

She never shared this obsession with anyone for fear they would try to stop her. After my workshop she took my suggestion and quietly began to write ten times each day: "I have everything I need today!"

A few days later some friends called and asked her if she wanted to go shopping. They went to the mall and looked at the new fall clothes. "Isn't that stunning!" said one of the friends. "Yes," she responded quietly, "but I have everything I need today." She couldn't believe those words came out of her mouth. She continued to write her affirmation until she had completed twenty-one days. In the end, she was able to talk about her addiction with her husband and, in time, put her finances back in order.

One way to find the right affirmation for yourself is to think about something you would like to change in your life, something you might want to add or let go. Close your eyes and imagine this goal as if it were real. Imagine the change has already happened for you. Now think of all the reasons why this change cannot occur. For example, perhaps you would like to be a model. You might tell yourself that you are too fat or not pretty enough. Now write a positive affirmation, turning around the negative statements that block you from making the change in your life. Make sure it has the five ingredients from the section before this one. It must be *positive, powerful,* in the *present moment, possible*, and *personal.* Your affirmation can be, "I am a beautiful and successful model today."

Perhaps you would like to spend more time in solitude, but think you don't have enough time. Your affirmation can be, "I have all the time I need to take some time for me today, " or, "God gives me all the time I need to take some time for me today." I often like including "God" or "all the energies of the universe" in my affirmations because that feels more powerful to me.

Affirmations help us to open up to positive energy and attract us to that which we would like to accomplish. They can be very powerfully combined with meditation. Make a tape of your affirmations. Meditate for as long as you wish and when you feel quiet and peaceful, play your tape. Affirmations are very effective when we hear them in a deeper state of consciousness, as we are when we are meditating.

I am terrific just the way I am!
All the energies of the universe are guiding me to my next step.
Solitude nurtures and delights my soul.
I am eating healthy food to keep me at a healthy weight.
I am loving and lovable. ▓

Pointing the Finger at Me

GO WITHIN YOUR OWN GROUND AND LEARN TO KNOW YOURSELF THERE.

❧ MEISTER ECKHART

I had been meditating for many years when I attended my first silent retreat, at Insight Meditation Society in Barre, Massachusetts. I arrived before five, hungry and tired, to hushed and excited whispers as the others arrived. The air was filled with energy and enthusiasm.

It was to be a very personal experience and out of respect for each person's privacy, we were told, we shouldn't look at anyone directly.

The meal that I expected at 5:00 P.M. turned out to be what was called "tea," consisting of a few types of crackers, rice cakes, honey, jam, and other toppings, including raisins and apples. Because Easter and Passover coincided this year, matzo was also a part of the menu.

I was starved! I peeked at others, trying to learn what would be appropriate to do. I assumed "they" all knew, while I didn't.

Finally, I settled on a piece of matzo and the fruit blend. Walking to an empty seat, my mind started: "This will never be enough. I'm going to be starved."

As I had taken so little it was gone in moments. I sat there very aware of my hunger and the long hours until breakfast.

Dare I go up and get some more? Then it came! Loud and clear! The old tape that I thought had gone away.

"What will 'they' think of me if I take a second helping?"

"Wait a minute," I answered. "I am here at a retreat for meditation and for rest. What do you mean by questioning what "they" will think?

I took a larger serving this time. Once again it was gone in no time. Dare I get more? A third helping?

"What would they think of me if I went up again?"

"Will they think I'm a pig?"

Suddenly a new question slowly began to come to me, a new and far more important question than "What will they think?"

That was the question I had learned so well from my mother who had asked it of herself all her life. I was really not sure I wanted to hear it because I knew the answer would change my life. Just knowing the question would change my life! I knew I could never be the same again, once I acknowledged it.

"What do I think?" That was the real question.

"Will I think I'm a pig? Could I be comfortable eating like a pig if I were alone."

I let myself feel everything. I examined the embarrassment, the shame, the fear of being seen as less than perfect, the fear of not having enough. I witnessed the wanting, the grasping, the hiding. I let it all sweep over me. I sat with me and let myself know me and experience my truth in a new light.

Slowly I rose and went back to the serving table. This time I really filled my plate, knowing all the time the lesson I was learning had nothing to do with anyone else. It had to do only with me.

It was about owning my own feelings and knowing they were okay. It was about seeing how I felt about things and not turning to others to make my decisions. It was about not denying my feelings, not resisting them, but experiencing them and watching them move away.

It was exactly what Insight Meditation represented. Insight. Self-knowledge.

The next night I had only two helpings at tea time.

Today I look to myself for my own truth. ❉

MINI-MENTAL RETREATS

> *THE MIRACLE COMES QUIETLY INTO THE MIND*
> *THAT STOPS AN INSTANT AND IS STILL.* ❈
>
> *A COURSE IN MIRACLES*

Guided Imageries

WHEN THE SOUL WISHES TO EXPERIENCE SOMETHING SHE
THROWS AN IMAGE OF THE EXPERIENCE OUT BEFORE HER
AND ENTERS INTO HER OWN IMAGE.

≫ MEISTER ECKHART

There are times when it really is impossible to get away by yourself. Maybe the babysitter canceled and you can't find another one. Perhaps there is a blizzard and your plane has been canceled. So many unexpected events can ruin the best plans.

Guided imageries are wonderful ways to take mini-vacation from what ever is going on in the outer world. Guided imageries, or visualizations as they are also called, are journeys we take in our minds. We can use our imaginations to take us to a pleasant place or to rehearse an upcoming event. Athletes use visualizations all the time to perfect their golf swings or watch themselves coming over the finish line first.

The imageries on the following pages can help you relax, meditate, let go of problems, and even love yourself. If you like, you can read them into a tape recorder and play them back to yourself whenever you wish.

To begin, find a quiet place away from any noise or interruptions. Sit in a comfortable position with your back as straight as possible. Make sure your clothing is loose and not binding. If you are in a chair, have your feet uncrossed and flat on the floor or you can sit on a cushion or directly on the floor with your legs crossed in the lotus position. Have your back as straight as possible. It's okay to lean against the wall. The only position not to use is to lie down, as that is conducive to falling asleep.

When meditating or doing a visualization we go into a deeper state of consciousness, so when you are finished count to five before you open your eyes so that you will come out slowly and gently.

It is so comforting to know that I have a place within me where I can always find peace. In just a few short moments I can go there, let myself relax, and let go of whatever is going on that might be creating stress in my life. ▓

Basic Meditation

AS THE BODY CAN FAIL ITS PURPOSE FOR LACK OF NOURISH-
MENT, SO CAN THE SOUL. . . . MEDITATION IS OUR STEP
INTO THE SUN.

❧ TWELVE STEPS AND TWELVE TRADITIONS OF
ALCOHOLICS ANONYMOUS

Close your eyes very gently and begin to breathe in and breathe out.
  Let your breath take on its own natural rhythm.
  Now...
  Let your entire body relax.
  Feel relaxation flowing from the top of your head
    all the way down to the bottom of your feet.
  Feel your scalp relaxing...
      your forehead...
      eyelids...
      the muscles around your eyes.

Relax your nose...
    sinuses...
    All the bones and muscles of your face.
Relax around your jaw, where we hold a lot of tension.
Now relax your mouth...
    chin...
    your throat.
Feel all your tension pouring down the back of your neck...
    poring down your shoulders.
    All tension and stress, anxiety, resistance, all negativity
    pouring down your arms...
    into your hands and fingers...
    into the tips of your fingers
    and completely leaving your body through the tips of
        your fingers.
Now relax your chest...
    diaphragm...
    all the knots and muscles of your stomach.
And let any stress you still might have pour
    down your spine...
    all stress and tension, fear, negativity
    feel it emptying down into the small of your back
    down through your hips...
    buttocks...
    thighs...
    down through your knees and legs...
    into your ankles...
    toes...
    into the tips of your toes...
    and completely leaving your body through the tips of
        your toes.
Now go back and check your body for any leftover
    tightness and bring relaxation to it.

And then return your attention to your breathing
    as you breathe in
    and you breathe out . . .
    as you breathe in
    and you breathe out.
Know that as you breathe in,
    you are breathing in powerful, positive energy.
You're breathing in peace
    and breathing out tension.
And as you breath out you are letting go of everything
    that is keeping you from feeling peace.
You are getting to know all the characteristics of your breath.
Now, sit quietly and be aware of your breathing.
Be aware of your breath
    as it goes in and as it goes out of your nose.
See if you can notice if it's cool or warm,
    long or short.
    Is it rough or smooth?
Don't change it. Just let it be and observe it as it is.
Notice if it's shallow or deep.
Notice if it changes.
If thoughts come in, just let them be and go back to your breathing.
If feelings come up, just notice them and go back to your breathing.
If you experience an itch or a pain, try not to move.
Bring your attention to that area of your body
    and watch it as it changes and moves away.
If you get lost in a thought or a daydream, just notice that you got lost and bring your attention back to your breathing.
It's helpful to make a mental note of what it was that took you away from your breathing.

Name it without judgment and then return to your breathing.

Know that as you are breathing in, you are continuing to fill with powerful, healing energy.

And as you breathe out you are exhaling everything negative that blocks you from feeling good.

Breathing in peace...

Breathing out tension...

Breathing in love...

Breathing out resentments...

Stay in this peaceful place for as long as you wish. And when you are ready to stop meditating, be sure to count to five and very slowly open your eyes.

I have all the time I need today to meditate. I have all the time I need today to improve my conscious contact with God. ▦

Finding Your Inner Sanctuary

YOU WILL REACH DOWN INTO YOUR MIND TO A NEW PLACE OF SAFETY. YOU WILL RECOGNIZE YOU HAVE REACHED IT IF YOU FIND A SENSE OF DEEP PEACE . . . HOWEVER BRIEFLY. LET GO OF ALL TRIVIAL THINGS THAT CHURN AND BUBBLE ON THE SURFACE OF YOUR MIND, AND REACH DOWN BELOW THEM. THERE IS A PLACE IN YOU WHERE THERE IS PERFECT PEACE. . . . THERE IS A PLACE IN YOU WHERE NOTHING IS IMPOSSIBLE. . . . THERE IS A PLACE IN YOU WHERE THE STRENGTH OF GOD, YOUR HIGHER POWER, LIVES.

ADAPTED FROM *A COURSE IN MIRACLES*

There is a very special place inside each and every one of us. It's a place where we are perfectly safe, a place where we can find peace. Take some time to think about how you would design a perfect place for yourself. It can be anywhere at all, near the ocean or the mountains, or the forest, or the desert, or anywhere at all. It can be a place you have already been or a brand-new place in your imagination.

Create a place in your imagination where you feel absolutely safe and really good about yourself. This is your special place. No one else can go here unless you invite them. It's a place where you find your truth, your answers.

Now meditate for a little while until you feel relaxed. Bring your full attention to your breathing, knowing that you're breathing in powerful, positive healing energy. Every time you breathe out, you're letting go of anything that is blocking your healing energy from coming in.

Let yourself see your inner sanctuary, your special place. Imagine you are walking to it now. Let yourself go deep within to your inner sanctuary. Take some time to use all your senses to know your special place. Do you hear any special sounds? Smell any special aromas? How does it feel beneath your fingers and beneath your feet? What time of year is it? What time of day?

Imagine you have everything you need here . . . everything you want. Create a place of comfort and joy.

Every time you breathe in, feel yourself filling with peace and as you breathe out, your are breathing out tension and anxiety. Feel peace flowing through your entire body. Spend some time letting yourself feel really good about yourself.

Know this is your special place, where you can always come to be alone and find solitude, where you can find peace.

Stay here as long as you wish and whenever you are ready, count to five before you open your eyes.

I am so grateful to know there is a deep place within me where I can always find peace.

God Bag Meditation

LETTING GO, MY HANDS ARE FREE TO GRAB ON TO LIFE.

ROKELLE LERNER

Begin by taking a few minutes to be with your breath, breathing in peace and breathing out tension. When you feel calm and relaxed, imagine that you are in your inner sanctuary.

In your mind create a beautiful bag. It can be made out of any material you wish. Design it with any color, size, or shape. Write the word "God" or "Higher Power," or any word that feels comfortable to you to describe a power greater than yourself. Add two handles to the bag.

Now think about a problem you haven't been able to solve or a situation about which you are unhappy or uncomfortable. Imagine that you have a pencil and piece of paper in your special place. Imagine yourself writing this down. Then, fold the paper and put it into your God Bag.

Step outside your special place, taking your God Bag with you, and look up, where you will see a magnificent hot air balloon hovering above you. Imagine it in any color and design that appeals to you. There is a string hanging from the balloon. Tie the string to the handles of your God bag and let go! Watch the balloon begin to rise, going higher and higher, up in the sky. See it becoming smaller and smaller until you can barely see it at all.

Let yourself feel lighter! Know that the balloon has taken your special problem or situation and that all the energies of the universe are now working on it for you. You will know what to do when the time is right. There's nothing else you have to do. Every time this situation comes up for you, just let it go, know that you have done all you can do at the moment.

Take some time to let yourself feel the peace and comfort of letting go. And whenever you are ready, come back to your room. Be sure you count to five before you open your eyes.

Whenever I have a situation I don't know how to handle, I can find peace by turning it over to God. Simply writing it down and putting it in my God Bag brings me closer to my Higher Power. Today I can let God be in charge of my life. 🎴

Metta Loving-Kindness

SO WATCH THE THOUGHT AND ITS WAYS WITH CARE, AND LET IT SPRING FROM LOVE, BORN OUT OF CONCERN FOR ALL BEINGS.

🌿 THE BUDDHA

Metta is a wonderful Buddhist practice that helps us to love ourselves and others and to bring forgiveness to ourselves and to others. It helps to free us of anger, resentments, self-doubt, guilt, and shame.

The word *metta* is a Pali word with two root meanings. One is *gentle* and the other is *friend*. Sharon Saltberg tells us that the foundation of Metta practice is how to be our own friend. She tells us that we must love ourselves before we can bring love to anyone else. Once we can bring love to ourselves, then we can expand upon that love and send love to others. It become possible, if we are willing, to send love to someone who has harmed us so that we can release ourselves from our anger and resentments. This is a wonderful exercise for forgiveness and freedom. Finally, we can send out this feeling of love to all people suffering in the universe. Jack Kornfield tells us, "The quality of loving kindness is the fertile soil out of which an integrated spiritual life can grow."

Begin by taking a few minutes to be with your breath, breathing in peace and breathing out tension. When you feel calm and relaxed, imagine that you are in your inner sanctuary. This is the place where you heart lives, a place where you feel love.

Say to yourself:

> May I be happy . . .
> > May I be peaceful . . .
> > > May I be free from suffering.

Now bring in someone into your heart who you care about and say:

> May you be happy . . .
> > May you be peaceful . . .
> > > May you be free from suffering.

Now if you want to, bring in someone you would like to forgive or receive forgiveness from, a person with whom you would like to come to peace and say:

> May you be happy . . .
> > May you be peaceful . . .
> > > May you be free from suffering.

Expand that feeling to everyone you know, your family, friends, and colleagues and say:

> May you be happy . . .
>> May you be peaceful . . .
>>> May you be free from suffering.

And now extend that feeling to people with AIDS, cancer, and other life-threatening diseases, to the addicts and the alcoholics, the hungry and the homeless, the people in wars and say:

> As we want to be happy, may everyone be happy . . .
>> As we want to be peaceful, may everyone be
>> peaceful . . .
>>> And as we want to be free from
>>> suffering, may everyone be free
>>> from suffering . . .

You can repeat these phrases over and over for as long as you like. Take some time to let yourself feel filled with the love you have brought to yourself and others. And whenever you are ready, come back to your room. Be sure you count to five before you open your eyes.

There are many variations of metta. Create your own phrases. For example, if you notice you are impatient, you might want to say, "May I be filled with patience." If you are having a difficult time with yourself, you can concentrate on bringing love into your own heart and say, "May I be filled with love." If you are angry at someone, you might say, "May I be free from resentments."

This is a wonderful exercise that you can practice in solitude for what is going on in your life at any particular time.

Today I have the willingness and the desire to be a loving person. I can take time in solitude to fill my heart with love and pass it on. ▩

CONTEMPLATION

ALL THE RICHEST WORDS IN THE LANGUAGE OPEN HIDDEN PASSAGES OF MEANING AND KNOWLEDGE. ❈

DEEPAK CHOPRA

Subject or No Subject

IT IS VITAL THAT WE GIVE OURSELVES THE TIME TO LISTEN TO OUR INNER WISDOM. NO PERSON CAN BE TOTALLY IN TOUCH WITH THE ABUNDANT KNOWLEDGE WITHIN WITHOUT TAKING TIME EACH DAY TO MEDITATE.

❧ LOUISE HAY

It was July 29. I looked up with surprise to see three red leaves at the top of a large, full green maple tree. I remembered only two days before seeing a single red maple on a path in the woods.

"That's not fair, God!" I heard myself saying. "It's only July 29. Summer still has a long way to go."

I laughed at myself. Who am I to question God? I thought. Life isn't fair in a lot of ways. Life isn't about my wanting summer to last. I'm only an infinitesimal part of it all.

I love to let my mind simply flow free, letting my eye catch the color of a tree, a passing dragonfly, a beautiful sunset. The song of a cardinal might pull me away from watching a ladybug crawl on a vine and suddenly I am in a different world, listening to a variety of songs and noises until a fly tickles my arm and I am brought back again. No worry thoughts. No mental storms. Just being wherever there is in the moment.

Alone, in contemplation, thoughts have a chance to surface. We can sit with them for a while and examine them. If they should pop into our minds when we are busy, they leave too quickly and we are caught up with whatever we are doing without the opportunity to give them any thought.

One form of solitude is contemplation. In many religions the goal of meditation is the contemplation of God. The doctrines or beliefs of the mystics is that it is possible to achieve communion with God and the knowledge of spiritual truths through contemplation.

We can explore metaphysical questions such as where do I fit into this universe? Is there such a thing as reincarnation? And the worldly ones such as does recycling really make sense? Not that we always receive answers simply because we take the time to sit with the questions. But we can get more in touch with life's mysteries. Author Lynn V. Andrews in her book *Love and Power* suggests that we invite the powers of the universe into our moments of contemplation, "so that the beauty that we are can sprout when a flood of energy comes, and the wisdom within us can be born."

We can focus on a particular issue, something that is going on in our lives, such as our job or a relationship. Or we can focus on a particular subject, such as integrity, purpose, or family. Or we can focus on nothing particular at all, letting in whatever comes up for us in our precious solitude, the gift of time we give ourselves.

Today is like no other day. I will trust my inner spirit to guide me, taking me wherever it wants me to go. I can focus on something particular or on nothing at all. I am free to be anywhere and stay or move on from there! ▓

The Contemplative Life

To ME, IT WAS AN ESCAPE FROM THE ARTIFICIALITY OF ILLUSION INTO THE RICHES OF REALITY.

*॰ PEACE PILGRIM

The contemplative life as followed by religious practitioners is one of withdrawal from the temporal world while enthusiastically entering that of the world of prayer, meditation, and service to God and humankind.

Fewer and fewer people seem to be called to this kind of life, but the ones who are show us a wonderful example of selflessness that seems out of step with what most people can manage.

Some years ago I was invited to a going-away party for a friend who had decided to join an Order of Religious Brothers who never left their friary and spent their time in worship and in manual labor to provide for their needs. My friend was around forty at the time and had struggled with his calling to enter the contemplative life since his youth. My thought was that he was receiving a wonderful gift from God and was giving to God all he had or was. He is still in the order, tucked away in the border area between the United States and Canada. I hear about him every once in a while and am glad to know he is happy and fulfilled at last.

Two other contemplative people who set such an example about doing their own thing while withdrawing from the world they had known were Helen and Scott Nearing, famous dropouts of the 1930s. They went to Vermont and started a farm for the purpose of supporting the lifestyle they chose. Their work was devoted to providing for their needs, creating a home, having time for their own intellectual pursuits, and visiting when there was time with the people they loved or who wanted to learn from them. Theirs was a much more temporal life, no prayer involved, but they wasted none of their natural talents and showed by their example that we can create and recreate ourselves as we choose.

We don't have to become nuns or monks, join a monastery, or even leave our home to have contemplation be a vital part of our everyday life. Taking time from our busy lives for contemplation is rewarding and peaceful. Reading, writing in our journals, and simply thinking can deepen our understanding of life. It can stretch our minds and our spirits as we reflect on a particular word or subject.

We can incorporate contemplation into a small portion of an active, stress-filled day to connect with our souls and slow us down to bring deeper meaning into our lives. Thomas Moore advises us that our souls "ask for some small measure of withdrawal from a world set up to ignore the soul." He adds that our soul, the "seat of the deepest emotions, can benefit greatly from the gifts of a vivid spiritual life and can suffer when it is deprived of them."

Contemplation helps us to make choices for the highest good for ourselves and others. To the extent that we reflect on decisions to be made or plans to be developed, we become mistresses of our own fate. Acting without reflection causes us to react to the circumstances around us rather than coming from the strength within us.

Today I am fulfilling the needs of my soul as I listen to that quiet voice within. I am taking time for reflection and contemplation. I am inspired by the wise words and thoughts that have been passed down through the ages.

Patience

DO NOT LOOK TO SMALL ADVANTAGES. DESIRING TO HAVE THINGS DONE QUICKLY PREVENTS THEM FROM BEING DONE THOROUGHLY. LOOKING AT SMALL ADVANTAGES PREVENTS GREAT THINGS FROM BEING ACCOMPLISHED.

❧ CONFUCIUS

As I was waiting at a gas station one day, I noticed an elderly man in a car parked off to the side, away from the pumps, tooting his horn. He shook his head in disgust, tooted his horn again, and shook his head yet again in disgust. In a few moments a woman, carrying a heavy shopping bag, walked over to the car. He leaned over and opened the door for her and she got into it. His look of disgust apparently came from her failure to respond quickly enough to his first toot. Then the man drove his car to the edge of the street and waited for a break in traffic before pulling out.

Another car waited just behind the first man. That driver, too, shook his head in disgust because the first driver was taking too long to pull out into the traffic. Impatience is a major factor in the stress we create in our own lives. It harms our bodies and depletes our immune systems. We want what we want, and we want it now! We want immediate gratification and find it difficult to tolerate waiting and not knowing. I read recently that people become impatient if they have to wait more than two minutes in a fast food restaurant because we are so used to having things right now.

We can see an extreme example of impatience when we look at some of the causes of wars. One country wants something right now and decides to go after it, right now. Their leaders do not have the patience to take the time to try to work things out with the other country.

Patience requires practice. We need to practice patience until it becomes a habit. We can learn it by being still and slowing down our life. We can practice patience while waiting for a traffic light to turn, by letting another car cut in before us, or while waiting in a long line in the supermarket.

One of the most simple ways to practice patience is by bringing your attention to your breath. Feel your breath as it goes in and out of your nose. You'll begin relaxing almost instantly. Remember that how you feel is your choice. You can choose to focus on whatever it is that is keeping you from doing what you want to do immediately. This will most likely set your face in a frown, keep your body tense, and make your breathing shallow. Or you can feel your breath filling and leaving your body. You can relax as your muscles release their stress. Hum a tune, write a poem, or watch a bird. We always have a choice.

We can practice patience by asking the following questions:

How important is it?
Must I have it right now?
Must I know right now?

Patience is a wonderful subject to contemplate in solitude. In what areas of your life can you see where you are impatient? Can you feel the connection between impatience, tension, and irritability in your body?

We can learn to be patient in solitude, by being still. We can let go and realize we are not in charge of the universe and that the world isn't centered around us.

Today I will sit quietly and let the world do what it wants to do. I don't need to act on my own or someone else's impatience. 🎗

Happiness

HAPPINESS ALWAYS WANTS TO BE SHARED. IT IS TOO MUCH.
IT CANNOT BE CONTAINED; LIKE THE FLOWER CANNOT
CONTAIN ITS FRAGRANCE, IT HAS TO BE RELEASED.

❧ THE BOOK OF WISDOM

My 5-year-old step-grandson Devin exudes love. Sometimes, while playing with his toys, lost in a world of his own, he suddenly becomes aware of his Grandma or me. He jumps up spontaneously, looks at one or both of us, and with a big grin says "I love you Gramma Sandy," and gives her a big hug and then says "I love you Gramma Ruth," and gives me a big hug. It seems as if all this love has come from way down in his toes, rising and bursting forth, too big to be contained. Something has moved inside of him and must be expressed.

One day his father came over to pick him up at the end of a day of visiting. The minute he his saw father, Devin jumped up with a huge grin, eyes filled to the brim with love, leaped into his father's arms, wrapping his legs around his waist, and as he is lept, yelled, "Dad! I love you!"

Such love and joy this boy expresses. If we could peel away all our layers of defenses, take off our armor, let go of all our fears and insecurities, and just be like a 5-year-old again, we too could experience such joy.

Abraham Lincoln believed "Most folks are about as happy as they make up their minds to be." When I first heard this I thought it was ridiculous. He certainly didn't understand someone like me, with all the problems I had in my life! That was many years ago and I have come to understand that happiness truly is a state of mind, a decision to let go of the pain and regrets from the past and fear of the future so that I can be fully in today.

Someone told me that the grand essentials of happiness are: something to do, something to love, and something to hope for. In Book I of the series *Conversations with God,* Neale Donald Walsch writes that "the soul is after the highest feeling of love you can imagine. . . .The highest feeling is the experience of unity with All That Is." He goes on to say that when you have a thought that is not in alignment with your higher vision, change it to a new thought.

Why not take some time in solitude to ask yourself questions such as:

> What does happiness mean to me?
> What makes me happy?
> Am I doing something with my life that makes
>   me feel truly happy?
> Do I have love in my life?
> Do I have a higher vision for my life?
> What am I looking forward to?

I am learning that I can change the thoughts that pull me down to thoughts that lift me up. I no longer let negative and fearful thinking block me from feeling joy and love. ✖

Finding Our Soul

FOUR THOUSAND VOLUMES OF METAPHYSICS WILL NOT
TEACH US WHAT THE SOUL IS.

✖ VOLTAIRE, EIGHTEEN-CENTURY FRENCH PHILOSOPHER

The word *soul* is a word and a concept that I have struggled for years to understand. I know I am not alone. Sages and mystics have contemplated these subjects ever since the written word has been recorded. Some ancient writings tell us they know exactly what the soul is, others tell us we will never know.

In the *Talmud*, written from 500 B.C. to 400 A.D. we are told we cannot see the soul or God. "Just as the soul sees but is not seen, so God sees but is not seen." And yet in the *Upanishads*, written in 800 B.C., we are given exact details. "The Soul is made of consciousness and mind; it is made of life and vision. It is made of the earth and the waters; it is made of air and space. It is made of light and darkness; it is made of desire and peace. It is made of anger and love; it is made of virtue and vice. It is made of all that is near; it is made of all that is afar. It is made of all."

Thomas Moore is a modern author. In his book *Care of the Soul*, published in 1992, he writes "Soul is not a thing, but a quality or a dimension of experiencing life and ourselves. It has to do with depth, value, relatedness, heart and personal substance." And "ancient philosophers taught that our own souls are inseparable from the world's soul and that both are found in the many things that make up our nature and our culture."

I have now come to know that I am connected to and am a part of God. In fact, God is everywhere and everything. Our souls are the very essence of who we are, our very spirit that is one with our Higher Power, with God.

I have read countless books in my attempt to come to some understanding of life and purpose. They help in the respect that they give me something to think about, to reflect on. But they do not give me answers. As we saw, one author tells me one thing while another author tells me the opposite. What and whom am I to believe?

This is where we must find our own understanding, come to our own truth, find what is right for ourselves. It is written in the *Bhagavad Gita*: "Know that which pervades the entire body is indestructible. No one is able to destroy the imperishable soul."

Although our souls cannot be destroyed, they can be ignored and then we have soul-sickness. We must take time to nurture our souls, to be gentle with our souls, and to listen to our souls. We need time out from all the chaos and noise and commitments. We cannot have a balanced, full, satisfying, and joyous life if we are too busy to honor our souls.

In another remarkable book, *Seat of the Soul*, Gary Zukav describes our soul as a positive, purposeful force at the core of our being. Can you feel a force driving you? Do you honor it? Is there something in your life that blocks that force? What is your deepest truth, the core of your being?

Now is the time for me to find my own answers to the very nature of my soul. Now is the time to discover what makes my heart smile and what makes my soul sing. ▨

The Power of Love

SOMEDAY, AFTER WE HAVE MASTERED THE WINDS, THE WAVES, THE TIDES AND GRAVITY, WE SHALL HARNESS FOR GOD THE ENERGIES OF LOVE. THEN, FOR THE SECOND TIME IN THE HISTORY OF THE WORLD, MAN WILL HAVE DISCOVERED FIRE.

TEILHARD DE CHARDIN

When I returned to graduate school in my late forties, afraid I was past the age of being able to learn, it was so exciting to discover I still had a mind and a memory. Every new book opened up new doors of information and challenge. It felt so good to have my mind stretched. There was so much to learn.

One teacher, John Grassi, was particulary stimulating and inspiring. I will never forget the day he put this quote by Teilhard de Chardin on the blackboard. The power of it stayed with me and I thought about it often over the years. My experience with recovery, graduate school, and meditation along with all the reading, workshops, conferences, and retreats I attended came together in it.

Over the years, love has taken on a whole new meaning, and I began to experience the power of love in an entirely different way. Mother Teresa said, "There is a net of love by which you can catch souls." This is what we were doing with the women recovering from alcoholism in our halfway house. We were loving them until they were able to love themselves. This is the love beyond romantic love. This is the love that can change lives. Mahatma Gandhi tell us that, "Love is the subtlest force in the world."

When we are young we need to be loved in a nurturing way. As we grow up, romantic love is what we long to experience. Most of us think that once we find it, everything will be perfect. We'll have everything we need. But the love beyond romantic love is spiritual love. Author Charles Whitfield once defined spirituality for me as our connection with ourselves, with others, and with God. Taking that definition one step further, I define spiritual love as the love for oneself, the love of others, and the love of God.

One day, when it was snowing, I walked over to the stairs very carefully, placing my hand on the railing as I took the first step down. I was aware that ever since I had broken my leg three years earlier, I no longer hurried down a flight of stairs without holding on to the rail. I was taking care of myself. I was loving myself.

Taking time for precious solitude fits into the category of self-love. It means I am taking care of myself. Only when I can love me can I feel good about myself. Then I can bring this love to others. Although we're always worthy of God's love, I don't always feel it, especially when I don't feel good about myself.

Take time in solitude to contemplate what loves means to you. Think about times when you have felt the power of love, whether you were the giver or the receiver of it. Remember the times when love has been withheld or times when you were not able to feel love or let love in.

I am learning more and more about me as I take time in solitude.Contemplating on the power of love brings me to a new understanding of my own power and the infinite possibilities I have for growth and happiness. ✖

Intentions

INHERENT IN EACH INTENTION IN THE MIND IS AN ENERGY POWERFUL ENOUGH TO BRING ABOUT SUBSEQUENT RESULTS.

❧ JOSEPH GOLDSTEIN AND JACK KORNFIELD

I remember the great excitement I felt when, many years ago, I read about the concept of intentions for the first time. To see the words in print that explained the way my life worked sent chills

through me. It was a very powerful moment. Up until then I had
followed an inner path, trying new things, turning this corner or
that corner, following an inner guidance I did not understand.

These words resonated truth. I never had words to describe
these feelings before. Intention is a mental quality that directly
proceeds an action or movement. Intention is the cause.
Movement is the effect.

In college I started a greeting card business. Years later I co-
founded an alcoholism treatment program for women. I just
knew I had to do these things. Both began with thoughts that
created energy to make something happen. My writing began
with the intention to share what I had learned with others.
When you think about it, it is possible to make almost anything
happen. We can't change the universe. We can't change other
people, but we can change ourselves and what we do with our
lives by our intentions. We can place a vision of our future in
our minds, a future that includes precious time just for ourselves, and make it happen.

We can make the following intentions or others of your
choice and the expected results will follow.

> We can intend to create a more balanced life for
> ourselves.
> We can intend to slow down, do less, and feel better.
> We can intend to improve our conscious contact
> with the God of our understanding,
> We can intend to make precious solitude a regular
> part of our lives.

*Today I am examining the areas I would like to change in my life
and creating intentions to make them happen!* ▓

Self-Discipline

SOME PEOPLE REGARD DISCIPLINE AS A CHORE.
FOR ME, IT IS A KIND OF ORDER THAT SETS ME FREE TO FLY.

❧ JULIE ANDREWS

Meditation and prayer are the only two disciplines that I never skip, no matter where I am or what is going on in my life. Not a single day goes by without taking this special time in the morning to be quiet, connect with the deepest part of me, finding that special place of stillness inside. Rarely do I hear any answers at that time. But later in the day or week or month I often have a inner sense of knowing what to do when I need to know the answers. This inner knowing has increased over the years.

Walking for my health is a different story. When I get away from my walking routine it might take me weeks to get back in the habit. Once I am walking regularly, I enjoy it and feel good about myself. But if a stretch of bad weather comes or I go out of town for a few days and don't walk, there I am again, struggling to get back. Beginning a new habit is one of the hardest things for me to do.

So how do we actually build time in our lives for solitude when we don't think we have the time? And perhaps even more difficult, how do we let ourselves take time for solitude when we think we don't deserve it, especially if we give everyone and everything else top priority?

It begins by changing our thinking. First we listen all the "buts," "ifs" and "whens" we tell ourselves. For example, we need to become aware and stop when we hear ourselves say, "I'll take time *when* the kids grow up", or "*If* I didn't have this demanding job," or "I'd like to *but* I can't find a minute." These are actually only opinions that we believe are truth.

Using affirmations is one of the best ways I know to turn these negative messages around to positive ones. Affirmations are simply positive statements we make to ourselves.

Here are some affirmations that can change your life:

> I deserve to take time for me today.
> I have all the time I need to do the important things in my life and still have time for me.
> I am worthy of my own special time to do in it whatever I wish.

I began my daily prayer routine. It took me five more years to add meditation to my life. Take time in solitude to contemplate your barriers to discipline and then consider the incredible possibilities of freedom and happiness discipline could bring to your life!

Today is a day to give up the struggle of resistance. I feel powerful energy flowing through me as I become willing to welcome discipline into my life! ▩

The Power of Words

WE RELY UPON THE POETS, THE PHILOSOPHERS, AND THE PLAY-WRIGHTS TO ARTICULATE WHAT MOST OF US CAN ONLY FEEL, IN JOY OR SORROW. THEY ILLUMINATE THE THOUGHTS FOR WHICH WE ONLY GROPE; THEY GIVE US THE STRENGTH AND BALM WE CANNOT FIND IN OURSELVES. WHENEVER I FEEL MY COURAGE WAVERING I RUSH TO THEM. THEY GIVE ME THE WISDOM OF ACCEPTANCE, THE WILL AND RESILIENCE TO PUSH ON.

✿ HELEN HAYES, *A GIFT OF JOY*, 1965

When I read something inspiring, I can actually feel a physical reaction in my body. Sometimes I get goose bumps when the words are deeply moving or they trigger a memory or they offer a truth I did not know I knew. I cry when I read something sad. Words can move us into and out of different emotions. Words can inspire us. Words can stimulate courage, pride, memories, sentiment, compassion, spirituality, empathy, tenderness, love, and much more.

There are occasions when we don't know what to do or where to turn. Sometimes just the right phrase or sentence can turn around a mood of depression or fear and lift our spirits. Many times we do not have the right words to describe what the many sensations are that pour over us. Some of us have old memories that have kept us stuck since childhood, frozen feelings that keep us blocked from moving forward. The right words can help us to express these feelings and to free us from their control.

It has been scientifically proven that words actually change the chemicals in our brain and the linings in our stomachs. Positive words stimulate our endorphins, the "feel-good" chemicals, sending these good feelings throughout our bodies.

Contemplate words such as love, faith, compassion, peace, generosity, ethics, forgiveness, purpose, or any other word that you wish to think about. What do these words mean to you at this time in your life? What do you feel when you read these words? Notice how your feelings change when you think of other words such as anger or resentment.

———————

Expanding Peace

WHEN ENOUGH OF US ARE AWARE OF SOMETHING, ALL OF US BECOME AWARE OF IT.

❧ KEN KEYES, JR.

One of the main reasons we seek solitude is to gain inner peace. We leave a world of busyness, demands, responsibilities, noise, and sometimes chaos to be alone, listen to the silence, and find serenity. We try to get in touch with ourselves.

Imagine what happens when you throw a pebble into a still pond. The force of the pebble landing on the water creates ripples that become wider and wider until they finally disappear and the water becomes smooth again.

There is also a ripple effect to the acquisition of peace in our journeys into solitude. When we return to our everyday life, we carry this peace with us. People around us often notice a difference in our moods and can be affected by it. As our lives change, so can the lives of those around us because our peace can be contagious. As the energy around us becomes more peaceful, others can feel it. As others take it on, they pass it on to people they meet and so on.

In his book *The Hundredth Monkey*, Ken Keyes, Jr., wrote about scientists who had been observing monkeys in the wild for thirty years. In 1952 on the island of Koshima they provided monkeys with sweet potatoes that they had dropped in sand. The monkeys liked the taste of the potatoes but found the sand unpleasant. One day an 18-month-old monkey named Imo washed the potatoes in a nearby stream. She taught the trick to her mother and her playmates, who taught it to their mothers. As the story is told, perhaps ninety-nine monkeys learned to wash their sweet potato between 1952 and 1958. One day the hundredth monkey learned to wash the potatoes. Suddenly, almost every monkey on the island began to wash their potatoes before eating them. The added energy of this hundredth monkey had somehow created an ideological breakthrough.

But more amazing, it was observed by the scientists that the habit of washing sweet potatoes had jumped over the sea, because the colonies of monkeys on other islands, as far as 500 miles away, began washing their sweet potatoes.

This phenomenon is known as *critical mass*. When a limited number of people know something in a new way, it remains the conscious property of only those people. But there is a point at which if only one more person tunes in to a new awareness, a field of energy is strengthened so that awareness of it is picked up by almost everyone.

Author Jack Kornfield teaches, "All other spiritual teachings are in vain if we cannot love. Even the most exalted states and the most exceptional spiritual accomplishments are unimportant if we cannot be happy in the most basic and ordinary ways, if, with our hearts, we cannot touch one another and the life we have been given."

As more and more of us make solitude a regular part of our lives, more and more people will be touched by our energies of peace and serenity. Imagine this ripple expanding throughout the world, touching everyone! What a beautiful world it will be!

It is so gratifying to know that as I seek peace and serenity for myself, I may be bringing peace and serenity to other people in my life. I am connected to all people who are a force of peace and light in the universe. ⚜

❧ ABOUT THE AUTHOR ❧

Ruth Fishel, MEd, CADAC, LMHC, is a therapist, retreat and workshop leader, and author of many books, including *The Journey Within, A Spiritual Path to Recovery*, a pioneer book on meditation, spirituality, and recovery, and the bestselling *Time for Joy*. She also teaches Stop! Do You Know You're Breathing, a program she developed for both individuals and teachers, nurses, counselors, therapists, physicians and psychiatrists to help their students, clients, and patients deal with stress, addictions, impulse control, anger, and violence. She has taught it nationally to thousands of people.

Ruth co-founded and co-directed Serenity, Inc., a multi-faceted nonprofit residential and outpatient treatment program for chemically dependent women from 1974-1988. Currently she is co-directing Spirithaven, Inc., a center that offers retreats, therapy, and meditation instruction for people in recovery and a wide variety of issues, which she co-founded in 1989.

Books
by Ruth Fishel

The Journey Within: A Spiritual Path to Recovery
Time for Joy, Daily Meditation and Affirmations
  (over 200,000 copies sold)
Time for Joy Daily Journal
Time for Thoughtfulness
Take Time for Yourself!
Cape Cod Memories

Newport Memories
Memories of the Florida Coast
Stop! Do You Know You're Breathing

Audiotapes

Time For Joy
You Can't Meditate Wrong
Transforming Your Past into Presents
Guided Exercises for Deepening Your Meditation Experience
The Journey Within
Discovering Your Source of Peace

For information on workshops and retreats, or to purchase books and tapes, call 508-420-5301, write to Spirithaven, 17 Pond Meadow Drive, Marstons Mills, MA 02648, e-mail spirithaven@neaccess.com, or go to www.spirithaven.com.